To Mary,

Who wants to lean
Not you! Nor I.
May this book increase the ache and
attainment of that for which / the
one for whom, we long.

— Dan

Assault on Eden

A Memoir of Communal Life in the Early '70s

Virginia Stem Owens

Baker Books

A Division of Baker Book House Co
Grand Rapids, Michigan 49516

© 1995 by Virginia Stem Owens

Published by Baker Books
a division of Baker Book House Company
P.O. Box 6287, Grand Rapids, MI 49516-6287

First published 1977 by Eerdmans under pseudonym. New 10-page preface by author.

Printed in the United States of America

Library of Congress Cataloging-in-Publication Data

Owens, Virginia Stem.
    Assault on Eden / Virginia Stem Owens.
        p.   cm.
    Originally published: Grand Rapids : Eerdmans, c1977.
        ISBN 0-8010-5241-6
    1. Owens, Virginia Stem. 2. Christian biography — New Mexico. 3.
Communal living — New Mexico. 4. Eden. 5. Sin, Original.
I. Title.
BR1725.095A3   1995
307.77'4'092—dc20
[B]   95-3452

Assault on Eden

Preface to the New Edition

What if you knew her
and found her dead on the ground?
How can you run when you know?

—Neil Young, "Ohio"

J wrote this book while I was recovering from an automobile accident in late 1975, as much as anything to explain to myself why two adults would take their two grade-school children away from a middle-class world of relative comfort and modest privilege to undertake, with little preparation and few resources, a life of subsistence farming on fifty borrowed New Mexico acres with ten other people even less suited to that life than themselves. And why this venture failed. Not just for the obvious reasons—under-capitalization, poor sanitation, lack of experience and discipline. I wanted to clarify what was wrong with our initial premises. The flaws in our underlying assumptions.

Not that we were an anomaly. In 1970, hundreds of thousands of young Americans—and many older ones—shared those assumptions. Communes were sprouting up all over, particularly in New Mexico, absorbing America's disaffected. Baba Ram Das and his followers were building the Lama Foundation on Wheeler Peak. New Buffalo was down the road in Arroyo Hondo. Just across the border in southern Colorado, Drop City cobbled a mesa with ungainly igloos called "zomes." A few years later, however, the great migration to the desert stopped. The emigrés packed up and went home or opened craft shops and became petty capitalists.

More years passed. The ship of state righted itself and sailed, if not serenely, at least stolidly ahead. Erstwhile hippies bought mutual funds. They *managed* mutual funds. Former protesters now worked for the government they previously denounced—one of them as its president.

At this point, we look back on those years reflectively, the way my parents reviewed World War II. Except the temper of those musings have been quite different. Where my parents pondered the turning point of their time soberly and even respectfully, the central crisis of my own generation's history is becoming the stuff of satire. Convictions that drove people to extreme measures—sacrificing jobs, renouncing citizenship, even risking imprisonment—are currently deconstructed and discounted. We accept as self-evident the conclusion that intelligent people never undertake quests that cost, that those who do so fail, and that those who did fail were merely fools.

I find this a painful betrayal of my own past. Like a family determined to keep its secrets in the closet, we're gradually revising the history of the late 1960s and early 1970s to justify replacing idealism with the bottom line, hungering and thirsting after righteousness with Total Quality Management.

When I wrote this book midway through the 1970s the worst seemed to be over for this country. Our troops were at long last out of Vietnam. Richard Nixon had resigned, and Gerald Ford had assured us that our "long national nightmare" was over. My husband and I, no longer impoverished hippies, were beginning new vocations in a rural parish southeast of Denver where he served as pastor and EMT while I wrote my first book. The seed planted at the end of this account had borne blessed fruit.

In 1976 we took our two daughters to the bicentennial celebration in a Colorado Springs park. The symphony played the *1812 Overture* while a thunderstorm rolled over Rampart Range to the west, adding lightning to the fireworks and thunder to cannons, as if the very forces of nature were validating this apotheosis of national concord. People who thought they'd never cheer for America again whooped and clapped and danced—bikers, grandmothers, hardhats, students—celebrating together after so long a drought of kindliness in the land. Everyone was glad to be united again, part of the same thing. A nation. A people.

Almost twenty years have gone by since that bicentennial celebration. College students no longer take over administration buildings. Their exemplar of radical politics is Ross Perot, not Huey Newton. At the 1994 replay of Woodstock the promoters focused on profit, not protest. The flower children have long since wilted, turned to compost, and been reborn as middle management. Yet despite our eagerness that evening to put away the past, settle down, and stick to business, the bicentennial good cheer dissipated almost as quickly as that summer thunderstorm.

Students are still being killed these days—but at high schools or junior highs rather than college campuses, and usually at the hands of their peers. And the conflict is likely to be over their upscale tennis shoes, not their political principles. The direction of their baseball caps advertises their drug retailer, not their ideology.

So what went wrong? If the war ended, Watergate was wrapped up, and the hippies got haircuts and returned to the workforce, why are our lives still so savage? This book begins with the biblical words that introduce the story of Noah and the ark: "Now the earth was corrupt in God's sight, and the earth was filled with violence." Violence is what never went away. Violence is what hasn't changed, what, in fact, has grown worse. The cause of that first watery apocalypse was the same scourge that drove us to the desert in the spring of 1970, fully expecting apocalypse in this country, anticipating a cosmic retribution for violence in Vietnam. And even then, the violence was already coming home.

The year before the events described in this book began, Richard Nixon had been inaugurated thirty-seventh president of the United States and commander-in-chief of the 541,000 American combat troops in Vietnam. A man with the improbable name of Sirhan Sirhan was tried and convicted of murdering Robert Kennedy. Lt. William Calley was ordered to stand trial for the massacre of civilians in a Vietnam village. Norman Mailer won the Pulitzer Prize for *Armies of the Night,* a "non-fiction novel" about the Chicago riots during the 1968 Democratic Convention. Sharon Tate and four friends were ritually murdered in her Los Angeles home by Charles Manson's Helter-Skelter gang.

At first, Americans who remembered the placid 1950s tried to comfort themselves with the notion that violence was occurring only in foreign lands or to public figures like politicians and movie stars. That it was perpetrated by foreigners or crazy people.

Then four students were shot on the campus of Kent State University in Ohio by National Guard troops. Normal Americans killing normal Americans. Our last illusion shattered. We reacted with horror and outrage. *What if you knew her and found her dead on the ground?* Neil Young asked, referring to nineteen-year-old Alison Krause in his song "Ohio." Four hundred forty-eight colleges and universities answered the question by shutting down that spring, closed by student strikes. Thousands of students didn't graduate on schedule that year. Thousands more threw away their credit hours, their tuition money. I still have a newspaper clipping with a picture of my husband returning his graduate assistant check to the university president rather than teach.

That May I sat one evening, along with hundreds of other teachers and students, holding a candle in the darkened quadrangle of a Missouri college where, till then, no anti-war protests had occurred. Nineteen years later I was reminded of that scene as I watched a sea of candles filling Wenceslas Square in Prague as the Soviet Union struggled in its death throes. The same kind of moral earnestness, the same depth of conviction, lighted both events.

The scenes in this book are illuminated in my memory not by the misty candleglow that blurs a moment of poignancy with nostalgia and softens its colors. Maybe because these events took place in the crystalline atmosphere of the Rockies' high altitudes, their images still come to me clear and hard-edged. As were our nation's divisions.

Rarely have so many been so morally affronted by those among whom they moved daily. Nations have hated nations, surely. It's easy, even relatively painless, to hate people you seldom if ever see. But during those years the enemy was your neighbor. Worse, your very family members. One side saw the other as cogs in the war machine. Pigs. Baby-burners. Stokers of the holocaust. The Establishment. The other side called their opponents anarchists, draft-dodgers, dopeheads, hippies. Everyone's righteousness-antennae quivered continually, alert for suspicious vibrations emanating from teachers, employers, grocery store clerks, baby-sitters, parents, children. The era's most popular bumper sticker—"America: Love It or Leave It"—encapsulated our alienation from one another.

We thought we were seeing the worst then—hundreds of thousands of otherwise orderly Americans taking to the streets, shouting slogans, burning draft cards. Police in riot gear responding with billy clubs, tear gas, and German shepherds. Body-bags from Vietnam. Naked children in flames. Thus, when the war ended, we assumed the worst was over. That the violence was finished.

Quite obviously, we were wrong. Violence, real and simulated, is still our chief concern. What has changed is the nature of the violence that afflicts us.

Certainly when we weigh Vietnam against our comparatively antiseptic incursions into Panama, Grenada, the Persian Gulf, and Haiti, no one can deny that our record overseas has improved. Also, the end of the Cold War, which descended like a gift from heaven, has delivered us from the threat of imminent nuclear destruction.

For America, however, that only means our violence is now completely homegrown. A domestic product. We can't blame the Communists or the Vietcong or outside agitators. We don't even have Richard Nixon to kick around anymore. We used to watch Vietnamese children fleeing for their lives on our television sets in the evening. Now the same news slots show American children trying to make it between home and school without being gunned down. Instead of field hospitals in the jungle, we now fund shelters for battered women. Rather than Green Berets we train child protection teams. The snipers shoot from our own freeway bridges, not some faraway hill with an unpronounceable name. The violence never went away; it simply came home to roost.

Our divisions in the 1960s and 1970s were clear and hard-edged. We all knew which side we were on. We could articulate our differences, name the enemy, even if it was only to call them "pigs" or "hippies." What name do we give the enemy now? To what faction does the fourteen-year-old belong who last month killed three people and then was murdered by his buddies to keep him from confessing to the police?

Is the enemy the two doctors killed at their Pensacola abortion clinic or the men who shot them? Did the million and a half women who used such clinics last year see their unborn children as the enemy? Is the bad guy Captain Joseph Hazelwood, drunk on the deck of the *Exxon Valdez* when it spread black gooey death in Prince William Sound? Or Jack Kevorkian and his Death Machine?

Is "the religious right" enemy or ally? And how do you know if you belong inside or outside that category? The lines that divide us today are not only much fuzzier than they were twenty-five years ago, but they have multiplied so rapidly that they form a fine mesh. So many and so poorly defined are the issues today that most of the time we don't even know whose side we're on. We can't explain ourselves or our positions—not to our opponents, not even to ourselves. During the 1960s and early 1970s our national conflict had the inexorable clarity of a Greek tragedy; now our strife seems as aimless and amorphous as an amoeba.

Left with no serious international adversary, we are being forced to look inward for the root of violence. So we have turned to blaming the 1960s and 1970s for our current social ills. It was Dr. Spock who produced a generation of irresponsible children and Betty Friedan who led women down the primrose path. But accusing the past is only our latest stratagem for externalizing our problem; we now seek to distance ourselves from it chronologically instead of geographically.

True enough, some unhealed wound from the past still festers. Some unfinished business keeps us from resolving the difficult questions the people in this book struggled with. Questions about sex, drugs, our place in the created order, the cost of community. As a people we are still not at peace about any of these puzzles. They have worked their way inward like unextracted shrapnel and all we have done is try to mask the pain.

This, I believe, is what went wrong: During the last quarter of this century it became physically impossible for American lips to shape the word "wrong." "Mistake" was as close as we could come.

When Richard Nixon climbed aboard that helicopter on the White House lawn in 1974, his V sign was all we got—not an apology. Though we were all relieved when the last U.S. plane left Vietnam a year later, we weren't happy. How could we rejoice at such a rout? The sight was both humiliating and heart-wrenching—

hands reaching out imploringly, mothers shoving their babies through aircraft doors in a desperate attempt to save them. If any soldier cried out "I'm sorry" as the plane lifted, the sound was covered by enemy artillery shelling Saigon. These images seared our national consciousness. Ever since then, guilt has been the enemy in American life.

Twenty years later we are a nation with no heroes but two hundred and fifty million victims. Betrayal of public trust, whether by government officials, pension-fund managers, or Marine Corps colonels, imputes no dishonor. Breaking private pledges imparts no shame. Plea-bargains and out-of-court settlements are now our two main methods of dispensing the best justice money can buy. Most divorces officially occur through "no fault" of anyone. Smokers with lung cancer and homosexuals or addicts with AIDS bear no responsibility for their diseases. No one fails in school.

Even the noble accomplishments of the Civil Rights movement in the 1960s are being undermined by our stubborn refusal to own up to iniquity. Did Martin Luther King really die just so Marion Barry could be mayor of Washington, D.C.?

Instead of either justice or forgiveness, we offer people support groups. For wife-beaters, rapists, child-molesters. Even the Roman Catholic Church, that heretofore reliable bastion of guilt, can no longer bring itself to utter the word "confession"; the new term, "Sacrament of Reconciliation," encourages communicants to skip over the sin that shattered their peace and fast-forward to the consolation. Today we would get Hitler together with Serbian leaders, Somali warlords, and Rwandan tribal leaders to talk out their ethnic-cleansing problems.

I titled the first edition of this book *Assault on Eden* because the people in it were desperately trying to recapture a state of innocence that would reverse the violence of the world and their own natures. We *believed* in apocalypse, retribution, a moral equivalent to the conservation principle in physics. As Crosby, Stills, Nash, and Young sang in their song about Woodstock, we wanted to get "back to the garden," the only safe haven in an apocalypse. We found out that attaining such a state takes more than just Jupiter aligning with Mars to unlock the garden gate.

We discovered something else as well—that renunciation is not the same as innocence. Turning our backs on this world didn't make us less guilty, just more poor. Nor could individual repentance absolve corporate guilt. Discovering this truth led some of our number to despair. Others kept searching for a way in. Some still are.

But though our original assault failed, we at least were clear about our objective. Eden's image was as bright and fair in our minds as it had been in Milton's when he wrote *Paradise Lost*.

That still remains the most important legacy of that era: a taste for paradise. The bright vision, which lacking, people perish. Our little collective on the banks of the Pecos may have overlooked the narrow entrance, no larger than the eye of a needle, to the Paradise we sought. But at least we were not ashamed of our desire.

We have had far too much ridicule of flower children, of naive hippies. To paraphrase that archetypal American pragmatist Ben Franklin, an ounce of naiveté is worth a pound of cynicism. If Vaclav Havel, after living out the apocalypse under first the Nazis and then the Communists, can still find the energy to work for the renewal of his country, then surely we can salvage something from the scrap heap of our own history. No one could call Havel naive. His patriotic statements are tempered by hard experience. "God," he says, "I don't know why—wanted me to be a Czech. It was not my choice. But I accept it, and I try to do something for my country because I live here." A modest statement. A humble claim that has none of the heightened rhetoric of our past. It is, after all, the meek who inherit the earth.

I realize that, whether we learn from it or not, history is not bound to, indeed cannot, repeat itself. I don't expect, don't even encourage, a resurgence of communes across the country. But surely we have not yet exhausted our moral imagination. What I long to see again in my own students' eyes is that same naked and undisguised hunger and thirst for righteousness that sent us into the desert twenty-five years ago.

1

Now the earth was corrupt in God's sight, and the earth was filled with violence.

—Genesis 6:11

"But don't you see that all these real leaps and destructions and escapes are only attempts to get back to Eden—to something we have had, to something at least we have heard of? Don't you see one only breaks the fence or shoots the moon in order to get home?"

—Innocent Smith in *Manalive* by G. K. Chesterton

The sodden Kansas skies give way to the high arches of the prairie vault held up along the highway by solitary storage spires where golden grain is poured on golden grain. The heart of America is a lonely place. Few folk feel strong enough to face that kind of space and sky. Those who live here are often contemptuous of the ones who eat the grain they harvest and store.

I am glad the rain has stopped, hot though it is. Perhaps the mattresses in the truck up ahead will dry out now. We roll on across the prairie, the kernel of our country. The pickup truck, twelve years old, bought for $250 from a midwestern farmer, is full of apartment-house furniture and secondhand garden tools found at auctions. High up over the cab, pointed forward like a ship's prow, is a hand plow. And the Volkswagen van I drive is full of packs and sleeping bags, seed flats and houseplants, two dogs and a big yellow cat, with people's arms and legs stuck in the odd crevices.

We camp that night on the outskirts of Liberal, Kansas, in a rest area, reenacting the westward flight forty years earlier of other nameless dispossessed. But we are fleeing from affluence, not poverty. In the dark we sing around our campfire, songs of railroad men, farmers, cowboys, wanderers—lives we've never known but which draw us. We know no plaintive songs of stenographers or students, bank tellers or computer programmers. That is why we are sleeping on the hard ground of Liberal, Kansas, and waking up with dew on our faces. Like the hero in the fairy tales, we have left home to seek our fortunes. But we know none of the songs of Zion, although we have often wept by the waters of Babylon.

Indeed, we flee across the Great Plains believing the very horsemen of the apocalypse are hot on our trail. *Babylon the Great has fallen, fallen.* We wonder that the people in the truck-stop cafe where we eat breakfast cannot hear the echo of that cry in the wind that blows dirt in their faces. The bodies at Kent State are barely in their graves. We are aliens in this country, in this very room. The road crew at the counter clot together over their coffee. Someone plays "Okie from Muskogee" on the jukebox. We affect an ease we do not feel. Then the two groups part on the plains, we heading west, they patching the black asphalt for us to travel on, each group discussing with avid attention to detail the sociological implication of the other. "Hippies. . . ." "Hardhats. . . ."

We climb into New Mexico with relief. At last we have escaped at least affluence. The virtue of poverty engulfs us. Even the vegetation is sparse and hard-won. Dirt houses surrounded by dirt yards. Few slick Safeways and Texacos, but gas pumps with inoperable, stinking rest rooms and roadside groceries. Yet out across the red raw earth are mesas of mystery floating in purple haze. A land aloof, yielding up nothing to support the glut of America.

The rise in the land is almost imperceptible to us, but not to our truck, now wheezing and balking its way up the steadily rising road. We hold our breath and sweat. How much further, how much longer? Will we make it? Finally, the last turn, the last stretch, just at dusk. The valley has been swept by a recent cloudburst. The land is grey and pale green, the river silver as we drop off into the valley. The wind is wet and fresh in our faces. Hope turns everything into a good omen. We park in the bare yard piled with drifts of tumbleweeds and dance around holding hands, delighted with our good fortune. We've made it back, back to our ramshackle Eden.

The reality of the place strikes us with solid force. Everything is only and exactly what it seems. No imitation carriage-house gaslight in the front yard, no aluminum-clapboard siding on the outside, no plasticized paneling on the inside. The house is adobe and no one has yet gone to the trouble of making imitation dirt.

The darkness that falls is also real, especially since the electricity has not yet been turned on. The solidity of real darkness confronts us as we search for the camping lantern and try to build a fire for supper. If the dry wood sticks splinters into us, what do we care? A drop of real blood oozes out, we marvel at the red beauty inside us, then wipe it carelessly, extravagantly away on our jeans.

That first night is full of strange disorientation. After we have eaten, washed the smoke from our faces, and hauled some of the mattresses from the truck into what looks like the soundest room, we pass around a joint to take the sharp edge off our travel weariness and then crawl under the sleeping bags to await what the light will bring us. We whisper and giggle back and forth like children, listening to the mice skittering in the dark around us. Their amazement at their new neighbors must almost equal ours.

My own disorientation is acute. "Where are we?" I keep asking my husband, Jack.

"In Moriah, New Mexico," he responds patiently.

"But that's just a name," I protest. "And besides, I don't know what 'Moriah, New Mexico' means."

"And I don't know what *you* mean," he groans wearily. "Go to sleep. Tomorrow we'll see where we are."

"But if you don't know where you are, you're lost," I continue. This all seems terribly important to me, although I realize it only sounds dumb to everyone else.

"You're not lost," Jack says in one last effort to reassure me. "Just hold on to me. I'm here."

But where is here, I want to know, though I restrain myself from asking out loud.

Our commune, New Mexico, our new life—they are all only a place in our heads. Is it the same place where we lie tonight? Do our minds' map and the land match?

I lie in the unfamiliar darkness and feel the mattress under me like a ship unmoored, drifting away. We are moving through the night, towards what dark shore none of us knows. *This* is what Robinson Crusoe felt. This is the meaning of shipwreck, not knowing where you are. I cling tightly to Jack. Jack is a place I know. There is at least a foothold here.

One thing is certain. There is no going back. What makes people do crazy things like this? Some have broken with their families, rejected their educations, given up jobs of at least a modicum of prestige and security. It is no small act to have come this far, wherever it is.

Those who glibly speak of "copping out" (called come-outerism in the nineteenth century) little know the desperation of those driven into the wilderness. It is escape from certain danger into the unknown. But as Tolkien said, the only one who despises escape is a jailer. One might as well have tried to persuade Noah to leave off building the ark and run for city councilman or set up a mental health clinic in Antediluvia as to talk to us about reforming the system from within. Like Noah, we are realists. No doubt "cop out" was one of the primeval epithets that assaulted the ark-builder, and we are equally oblivious to it. Let the fools beat their bourgeois brains out against the crumbling wall of reform. Somehow they all end up wearing the same clothes and carrying the same credit cards as the oppressors. The mark of the beast, as far as we are concerned, is dispensed by IBM computer printouts.

Apocalypse, apocalypse. How often the word is in our mouths. The end, doom, destruction. Wrath and justice are combined for us with the same alchemy that kindled the hot desire for vindication in the captive Jews and the Christians under Domitian. We have a horror of violence and will not ourselves aid the destruction of a system doomed to fall under its own weight of evil, but neither do we intend to stand in the way of any scourge of God. We cheer on the avenging angel.

All America is, in the summer of 1970, in the same sad shape as the "burned-over district" of New York State in the 1820s.

Socialistic and communitarian theories reinforced literalistic concern for the early Christian communism described in the New Testament (Acts 2:41–47). Mysticism and various forms of pantheism provided links to important philosophic trends of the time. Other interests, often with only remote Christian rootage or none at all, kept appearing and reappearing in different contexts. The discovery and popularization of "animal magnetism" (hypnotism) added a new dimension to popular conceptions of human consciousness. Lurking under America's puritanic Victorianism was a persistent and not sufficiently appreciated restiveness about sex and the monogamous family. . . .

(Sydney E. Ahlstrom, *A Religious History of the American People*, p. 477)

This heritage of the insatiable religious quest burns in our American bones. A century and a half later, the refurbished panaceas of religious gurus are still considered entertaining enough for prime-time television.

The historical undercurrents of our own experiment come from many tributaries, though we are ignorant of most of them. For instance, there is something of Joseph Smith and Nauvoo in our midst. If we cannot swallow the unsophisticated Book of Mormon, neither can we let go that dark and bloody irrationalism that fosters paranoia and invites persecution. We too have our own "special revelations," whether they be from Edgar Cayce or Paul Ehrlich. Cast in the mystic or the scientific metaphor, it makes little difference. All signs point toward The End. We all expect the disintegration of American society and that it will be in one way or another violent. Our one hope is that there will be a saving remnant and we will be a part of it.

"I am like a huge, rough stone," proclaimed Joseph Smith, "rolling down from a high mountain; and the only polishing I get is when some corner gets rubbed off by coming in contact with something else, striking with accelerated force against religious bigotry, priest-craft, lawyer-craft, doctor-craft, lying editors, suborned judges and jurors, and the authority of perjured exec-utives, backed by mobs, blasphemers, licentious and corrupt men and women—all hell knocking off a cor-ner here and a corner there. Thus will I become a pol-ished shaft in the quiver of the Almighty, who will give me dominion over all and every one of them, when their refuge of lies shall fail, and their hiding place shall be destroyed."

But there is also more than a bit of Brook Farm in us. The educated's love of discourse: problematic, hypothet-ical, analytical. The "Plan of the West Roxbury Com-munity," published in that nineteenth-century voice of the avant garde, *The Dial,* in January of 1842, could have come hot off the underground press of 1970, except for a few genteel curlicues here and there, and could easily have gained the unanimous approval of our group:

A few individuals, who, unknown to each other, under different disciplines of life, reacting from different social evils, but aiming at the same object—of being wholly true to their natures as men and women, have been made ac-quainted with one another, and have determined to be-come the Faculty of the Embryo University.

In order to live a religious and moral life worthy the name, they feel it is necessary to come out in some de-gree from the world, and to form themselves into a com-munity of property, so far as to exclude competition and the ordinary rules of trade. . . . They have bought a farm, in order to make agriculture the basis of their life, it being the most direct and simple in relation to nature.

A true life, although it aims beyond the highest star, is redolent of the healthy earth. The perfume of clover lingers about it. The lowing of cattle is the natural bass to the melody of human voices. . . .

The community aims to be rich, not in the metallic representative of wealth, but in the wealth itself, which money should represent; namely, LEISURE TO LIVE IN ALL THE FACULTIES OF THE SOUL.

High-flown sentiments, easy enough to ridicule. The natural bass of the lowing cattle lost its charm when Hawthorne confronted the manure pile, about which the perfume of clover decidedly did not linger. But after the dream has dwindled through ridicule, think how powerful the compulsion must be to drive people to stake their lives on such a slender spider web of a dream. All the history made in America was by such desperate people wagering upon a desperate dream.

Like the Faculty of the Embryo University, most of us here have at least some college education. What kind of culture is it that offers openhandedly the best fruits of its civilization only to have them spurned? Many among us could never have read the books we have or ingested our ideas in any other time or place. But if one has "every opportunity," the opportunity one chooses is likely to be the unlikely, the unusual. Joseph Smith, uneducated and unpropertied, had not had every opportunity. Like a water course bursting through the only narrow opening available to it, his movement was swift and strong. But the folks at Brook Farm came and went, discussing Kant and Transcendentalism, notions much too evanescent for the "King of the kingdom of God." The summer of 1844 saw the martyring of the Mormons and the dwindling of Brook Farm, just as the summer of 1970 saw the Kent State deaths and the withering of flower power.

Perhaps not religion but education is the opiate of the people. Who will die for philosophical speculation? Not even Galileo.

Like the Brook Farmers, we too are dilettantes. They dabbled in the Shakers and the Rappites; we stock our library with Zen and Baba Ram Das.

What a sad hybrid we are! Whatever our affinities with Brook Farm, that experiment aimed at being a utopia, while we will settle for nothing short of paradise. Utopias bore us. There is no mighty vindication, no justice and wrath in the coming of a Utopia, only a "re-education." Give us a good, resounding apocalypse, full of the crashes of capitalism, the wailing and gnashing of Nixon's teeth, the fumes of the military-industrial complex rising like incense. And then. . . .

The picture dissolves, the transition is unclear, but suddenly there we are: innocent, strong, loving. Every step in harmony with the great cosmic dance. A delirious vision to which we are all devoted. It is no great concern that the transition is unclear. Like all good children brought up on Walt Disney, we believe that if you wish for something hard enough, it is bound to come true. At present we are only interested in the first vision. Paradise will have to wait till tomorrow.

But tomorrow does come, and in the light of morning our paradise seems disguised as a desert, made green only here and there in strips of irrigated alfalfa and in need of quite a few repairs. Crumbling adobe sifts down through the cracking plaster. Windows are broken out. Judging from the eroded walls, the roof leaks in many places.

Still, opening our eyes to a sun whose light is more immediately present than we are used to is intoxicating. It has already climbed over the mesa that lies to the east of our house, and the rest of the world—insects, birds, air currents, even the solitary neighboring farmer—is responding to the light. Eager to become a part of this busy, buzzing natural world, we hurry outside, stretch and yawn broadly, and begin unloading the truck and van.

New ventures, though, are never propelled by only a corporate vision, I think. There must be that if ever a group of people are to act together, but who knows what private yearnings held the people individually to that stake in Nauvoo or kept even the dilettantes at Brook Farm for their season's stay? We have Hawthorne's account in *The Blithedale Romance* of his observations of certain characters, including his own, in this romantic and tragic interlude. Though they all ascribe openly to that intoxicating dream of "brotherhood," each one has some secret, sometimes even unconscious, reason for acting out the dream: ambition, pride, guilt, desire to be loved, to foster a family, to be provided with an identity.

And we are no different. Amongst the bundles and bedding, the furniture, the garden tools, the pets, we have brought with us our own hidden desires, our private dreams. We want Paradise in the particular. Our own Adam or Eve, a bower, ways to fill our days.

Faye, for example, who sings almost constantly, plays the flute beside the campfire at night, and shuffles around in a queer, private dance, is voracious for excitement. Some interior drama, like her dance, accompanies her everywhere, preparing a role for every situation. She even buys dramatically outdated clothes at thrift stores to dress up for her part. This westward-moving caravan, leaving the island of the university campus just as it has been closed by a student strike, is exactly the thing to capture Faye's imagination. A hundred years earlier she would have been a dance hall girl, a riverboat gambler, an explorer, Mother Ann Lee. Now she is Faye, girl-communitarian, free spirit, hitchhiker.

If Faye is seeking excitement, Wayne is seeking security. Where she branches out, he wants to take root. He's not a drifter, but a settler. This venture provides him with a place to settle, to build on, build up, work, care for. Broad-shouldered and brooding, he also needs someone to work and care for, someone to share his vision with. An unwieldy combination of old-fashioned, homespun virtues in a culture where they only work in TV westerns. So to counter that culture, Wayne has joined this new settlement. Maybe this is the place where he can get on with his dream.

Sally is a bright young career woman who can find no meaningful job in straight society. Independent and creative, she would, ideally, like a loom, a weaving shop. Friends she can rely on. A surrogate family in which her childlike whimsies can have full play. Other children to whom she can tell her funny little stories, peopled with creatures from her imagination. She makes up adventurous life histories for all our pets and adds to them weekly. But her spirit has been worn dangerously thin in places. She, Faye, and Wayne have all lost their fathers, Sally only recently. For her the wound is still fresh. She is illness-prone, and many of us feel an unvoiced dread that Sally, tough and resilient as she seems, is more vulnerable than most to whatever malevolent spirits lurk about.

Daniel, like his nineteenth-century mentor Thoreau, is unencumbered with the kind of personal involvements that would get in the way of his experiments with life. He has inherited his hero's passion for analysis. Trained as an architect, he has already been in the Peace Corps in the Far East and in the army in Korea. Now he has set aside time to explore "alternative lifestyles." He wants to discover, in the classical sense, "the way to live." Not impulsive or romantic like the rest of us, he seeks order, balance.

Lillian is quite purposefully starting a new life. An academic career and a marriage to which she has given six years of her life have just disintegrated. She is determined that she has worn out her last rut. A new life, one shaped by her own quite capable hands, something daring and un-mousey, is what she wants. And other people around to keep up her spirits. But never again will she depend on a person who can betray her. Lillian has only just discovered that the world is full of cabbages and kings, and she means to explore them all.

This is only a sample of the personal needs brought to these fifty arid acres and the ramshackle adobe farmhouse. Sometimes as many as seventeen secret worlds bumped up against one another there. And who knows what other unspoken yearnings drove people— young, intelligent, educated, with every advantage their parents dreamed of—into the desert to take up a barbaric life? In a way, the public, corporate articulations of our goals, couched primarily in political rhetoric, were an amalgam of all our private disappointments with life in mainstream society.

Like Noah, we lived amongst violence. Our land knew no excitement but in violence, no peace or place to settle, only unreasoning and virulent family scenes, disorder and imbalance, desertion, despair. The more mythic elements of our country's violence were being exported to a foreign setting in Vietnam to be staged for the daily television ritual. It was this violence, on every level, that we sought to flee. Yet it was not the ark we wanted to build, that small, stifling temporary place of waiting for the fulfillment of the promise. We were impatient for Paradise. So ignoring the cherubim and the flaming sword, we plotted to storm the gates of Eden.

2

And the eyes of the two were opened, and they knew that they were naked.

—Genesis 3:7

If the jewel which every one desired to possess lay far out on a frozen lake where the ice was very thin, watched over by the danger of death, while, closer in, the ice was perfectly safe, then in a passionate age the crowds would applaud the courage of the man who ventured out. . . . But in an age without passion, in a reflective age, it would be otherwise. People would think each other clever in agreeing that it was unreasonable and not even worthwhile to venture out so far.

—Kierkegaard, *The Present Age*

July 4, 1970. We start off the day playing the "Hallelujah Chorus" into the sleeping ear of Bob, whose birthday it is. Everyone is struck by the irony of the situation. The birthday of the country we both love and hate. Bob's birthday. Bob, whose father is a U.S. senator.

Bob is only recently out of a mental hospital where he spent his adolescence. Being antisocial—that is, preferring animals to people—he was an embarrassment to his father's political career. Bob has a big orange cat without a tail who tolerates only Bob touching him.

The cat catches rabbits in the night and we hear them scream.

I am puzzled that Bob was diagnosed as antisocial, although he confirms that at the time it was an accurate description. He is more rarely morose than any of us. He is both talkative and articulate. He sometimes worries about his relationship to women, but he is, after all, only eighteen today. Spoiled by too much money. His brain perhaps a little wacky from incredible amounts of home-brew drugs concocted in the hospital. He can recite entire albums of Firesign

Theatre. We are all exasperated by him, yet dote on him.

Everything moves like molasses in the mornings. Discipline is a dirty word in this crumbling adobe house, built by some unknown Spanish/Indian before the land it sits on ever became a part of the country whose birthday, along with Bob's, we are gradually gearing up to celebrate. Its present inhabitants use incomprehensibly stupid phrases like "doing my own thing" in a six-room house that holds from seven to eighteen people, has no bathroom, a leaky roof, broken windows, and one cold-water spigot whose purity no one checks and which eventually gives us all paratyphoid.

No one enjoys the disorder and dirt. We are all more or less uncomfortable with the chaos. Yet some secretly know that this is only temporary for them and thus escape the panic the rest of us feel over the huge droning flies and the crud that creeps further from the corner of the kitchen daily.

Finally things coalesce enough to get breakfast fixed. Ninety-five percent of the cooking is done by the women; the other five percent by Bob, who enjoys making his specialty dishes. Another example of the astounding gap between rhetoric and reality that none of us is prepared to deal with.

Bob's honorary birthday breakfast is served in bed. He gets toast and eggs. The rest of us eat boiled brown wheat berries, part of the hundred-pound sack we bought on our way through Kansas to New Mexico. They are hard to cook and hard to eat, but no one complains, teeth grinding away on those indomitable grains, soaking in the thin dried milk and honey. No one would exchange his bowl for one of Sugar Snacks, but we all envy Bob his eggs.

By the time the dishes have been sulked over by who-ever's turn it is (dishwashing is our sole attempt at a work schedule), it is almost noon, and we turn to the celebration of the day. Imported by our latest midwestern immigrant are ten caps of psilocybin. As always, intricate details of distribution must be worked out with great care, many of them ethical questions. In this there is no floundering: there are no outside experts, no appeal to authority other than the seniority within our own group. *We* are the authorities and we approach the subject with analytic rigor.

Should everyone drop? At the same time? Should the chemical be allotted according to body weight, tolerance, or request? Should we all stay together? Who will look after any problems that develop? Who will deal with outsiders, should they appear? Jack and I have two little girls. Who will take care of them?

As it turns out, we drop at staggered times. A couple of people don't drop at all, so there is plenty to go around, all of us taking what we decide we can handle.

It is only around psychedelics that we become a true community, even tribal. There is never any hoarding of dope. We never are floating in the stuff, but whatever we have is shared among us all. It is the basis of most of our celebrations—like cocktail parties, only homelier. It clarifies our rift with society, thus drawing us, despite our other failures, closer together.

There is some concern about the quality of the psilocybin, which after all is not covered by the FDA, so a few of the hardiest go first to try it out. The women are whipping up covered dishes for the final event of the day—a picnic on the rocks and cliff down by the river. By one o'clock everyone has ingested at least half a cap of psilocybin and we start for the river, half a mile away.

The sonorro, over which in innocent awe we continually wander, both stoned and straight, provides the best of our lives here. In it we are closest to realizing what we have come here for. Here—outside the society we have fled, outside ourselves—is a world of such integrity and harmony that we stumble along, fondling the rocks, smelling the juniper, waiting for a message, sure that if we have a home on this earth we would like it to be the way the stones here have homes. As soon as we cross the irrigation ditch in front of the house we face half a mile of unbroken silence and sun to the river over a ground whose holiness we do not understand but sense.

Somehow we have managed to stray from one another and are now scattered in small clusters across the sonorro. I have a flash of how incongruous we would look to a passing helicopter. The chemicals have begun to clamp down; it descends with a rush, that feeling of lack of control, so intriguing to the Western mind. Something else is in control—karma, the desert, God. We don't really know, but we are sure it's not ourselves. We wait to see where, literally, the spirit will move us.

Jack and I are at the sandy bottom of an arroyo beside a big cottonwood. I have two problems to work on: the constant nausea produced by the chemicals and the way the lines in the rocks keep becoming snakes. Not that I am afraid of them. I simply realize that there is a practical necessity to distinguish the rock snakes from real snakes. We feel close and comfortable in our small oasis. Jack says not to worry, that he will take care of me. I believe him. We make love at the foot of the cottonwood, both from sheer delight in one another and because we've read it is impossible under these conditions.

Afterwards we face the now gigantic task of getting to the river. It seems that as soon as we get settled in one place, there is always the irritation of having to move on. We realize that our perspective has shifted: objectively it is no more than a ten-minute walk to the river, yet the distance has assumed the proportions of a trail drive across the plains. It is Christopher Robin's expedition to the North Pole. This double vision amuses us greatly, but our amusement does not evaporate the huge reality. The shade of the tree shifts over the sand as the wind blows, replacing shadow with light and back again. It all seems a marvel. We talk about our parents, how our love for them and theirs for us is some- how missing a vital connection. It all seems a great waste. A tangible wave of pity sweeps over us and we cry for a while. Then it seems time to move on.

Out from under the dappled shade of the cottonwood, down through the arroyo, stained purple and gold and pale green. The colors are real, part of the audacity of the desert. The patterns they make are the games our minds are playing with us. We climb the soft side of the arroyo onto the top of the plain again, picking our way among the rock and cactus, concentrating hard on avoiding the spikes of Spanish sword that stud this vast fakir's couch. Up ahead is a high knoll where others are already scrambling at various levels. Gradually every- one is converging on this high point from which we can see the flood plain, a village a few miles away, our own house behind us, and overhead a hawk wheeling.

We feel some small panic, scrambling to the top of the rocks. My bone-deep desire to stay put in one place, not to have to move again, is in constant tension with the flow going on around me. Necessity—to stay with the others, to get to the place of meeting, to be where the food is at the right time—inexorably drives us on, when I want so desperately to be still. There is partial satisfaction in each way station of the trip, but what I long for is reaching a place I won't have to move from. I know that once I get to the top of the knoll I won't have to move again, at least for a while. Therefore, bridging the gap between where I am now and the place I want to be makes the desire to compress time acute. I want to *already* be there. The seconds to the top seem interminable, but finally we are there and again in the midst of our friends. It seems a very long time since we last saw each other, and we are full of congratulations for the success of the trip so far.

Some are examining marks on the rocks they think are Indian petroglyphs, and Bob begins to make up an elaborate tale about how they came to be there. He is only a little wackier stoned than straight. I lean back against a dark granite boulder, fighting off nausea and thinking how crazy we all are. Yet the experience doesn't seem at all unnatural.

Later, when we have all scrambled down the far side of the rocks and descended into the riverbed itself, Jack and I wander upstream around a bend. The river is low, only ankle deep in most places. We marvel at the smooth, water-worn stones, the way they fit the curve of the water. The wet satiny sand gives way softly beneath our feet. A big boulder further upstream looks like the prow of a ship sticking up out of the water. It becomes another way station in my mind, like the cottonwood tree and the top of the rocky knoll, where I can rest for a while. We wade out to it and I crawl up on top and lie back with relief. After I assure

Jack that I will be all right alone for a while, he goes off on some private exploration.

The silence and the water lap up around my rock. Overhead in the gap of tremulous blue sky left between the cliff walls, which rise sharply on both sides of the river here, the clouds move by. Clouds such as I have never seen before. It is not the old game of seeing shapes in clouds, which tends to flatten them out against a background. Strangely, it never occurs to me to see them that way today. What I am most keenly aware of is the depth, the dimensions of the clouds. They do not sail along like ships, but roll and tumble in wide, slow arcs as they move across the roof of the canyon. Nor do they coagulate and disperse into wisps. There is merely a certain spectrum of light in which they are visible to my eyes, and they move in and out through that spectrum. When they reach a certain height or depth they simply fade through the limits of perception, like the Cheshire cat disappearing bit by bit.

It is the purest, most fascinating spectacle I have ever witnessed. I could watch forever and never grow tired. Also I am quite sure that up on the level where the clouds are turning and tumbling in fantastic spirals and pirouettes, there is music they are dancing to. Stately, majestic cloud-music that I can almost hear, can even feel the vibrations of tingling my ears. It's the kind of enhanced vision you only expect from movies, but with no gimmicks, no end. No "That's all folks!" written across the sky, no lists of credits. The clouds will continue to dance whether or not anyone is there to watch them. This is infinitely satisfying.

When at last Jack returns and says it is time we started moving back downstream where the others are, I am still so fascinated by the clouds that I am mildly impatient with anything that takes my attention away from them. I would like to make the trip floating on my back so as not to miss any of the high spectacle. As it is, all I can do is insist that we stop every few yards so I can look up and see to what point they have progressed.

We make one long stop beside a grassy bank where a seep spring trickles down into the river. This land is full of surprises. Dry, overgrazed for years, its chalky bones exposed daily to the domineering sun, it does offer a few tucked-away secret spots where enough water collects to make familiar green life possible. Along the trickle are lush emerald grass and even tiny flowers. A few feet below, the red, raw river runs. Up above, the sonorro bakes in the sun. But here, in an out-of-the-way wrinkle, is a miniature meadow.

As we sit gazing down the river, we see a figure leaping and zigzagging back and forth across a broad sandbar. Her hair is flying out behind her as she laughs and splashes. We come closer and see that it is our ten-year-old, playing at being a river sprite. We sit on our heels and watch her, dancing as the clouds danced, something entirely outside ourselves. She has tied onto herself every available colored scarf she could find at the house, and now she is making them all flutter and dance around her like feathers and flames. I feel a relief much like the one I felt about the clouds. Just as they would continue their solemn rolling way across the sky whether I was there or not, so she will exist, be a person, with or without me.

If this sounds like a desire to be quit of responsibility, it is not. I definitely *do* want to be there, just as I wanted to go on watching the clouds forever. I simply realize at this moment that I do not hold this person in existence. Some other power outside of me makes her tie colored scarves to her brown little body and dance by the river. I am only background, like the sky to the clouds.

We come out of our hiding place and she calls to us to hurry. The picnic is ready now. Indeed the afternoon is stretching thin out across the flood plain. It has been several hours since we left the house.

We take a path up from the river onto a high, flat cliff that extends precariously over the water. Back away from the eroded cliff edge in the ruins of an adobe hut, built and abandoned by an unknown settler, the food is spread out. A black iron pot of beans, a casserole full of rice spiked with whatever tidbits could be found in the kitchen, a sesame cake, tortillas, salad from our meager garden, and Kool-Aid. Everyone is in good spirits. The scene reminds me, incongruously enough, of church picnics, fishing camps by the river, family reunions. It is much closer to these than to the backyard barbecues of the suburbs. A regular old-fashioned Fourth of July. And then, as the sun falls and our campfire lights up our faces, it is more like being refugees, stopping for a while on a long trek to an unknown destination. The darkness is close and comfortable.

For several days Bob has been working on some special fireworks for the occasion. Explosives had been part of his antisocial behavior, starting with his first junior chemistry set. After everyone has eaten and settled back into the summer darkness, he sets up his display, a series of rockets aimed out across the river to the sandy flood plain far down on the other side. They are big and noisy but haven't the colored showers of sparks I had been hoping for. When they are spent, we discover our own makeshift variety. Setting fire to the ends of driftwood sticks, we twirl them in patterns through the black velvet night. The glowing ends make pale colored streaks that seem to hang in the air like whirling wheels. When the dervish operating the stick gets wound up enough, he flings it out across the arching sky to the river, its flame making a long luminous rainbow in the night. The colors linger long enough, at least on our retinas, for everyone to exhale a long "ahhh" at the spectacle. Some of us simply sit and watch as others develop more and more complicated patterns. This is real fireworks.

At last someone realizes that it is getting too cold to stay up on the cliff much longer. When the sun goes down behind the foothills the heat drains quickly from the desert. We collect the pots and pans and start the trek back to the house.

Half a mile across a sonorro at night is quite different from the same distance by day. The moon has risen like a giant floodlight, making the plain below into an immense stage setting. We wander up and over rises, into and down arroyos, scrambling up the sides again. On one comparatively flat place we pause for a trucking demonstration. Trucking, that inexplicably hilarious comic-book walk, somewhat akin to a vaudeville stroll, is meant to accentuate our absurdity in the world. One leans as far back as gravity allows and reaches gingerly forward with each foot, pumping the arms in time. Some among us have developed it to the point of art, like Charlie Chaplin's penguin waddle.

We often see our place in the world through the filter of movies or comic strips. Nature we can take straight. Its coherence and integrity is so great as to command even our desiccated sense of respect and awe. We can simply sit quietly and look, but all the time knowing that we ourselves do not participate in that coherence and integrity. We can only be observers. The moment we move or open our mouths, our outsideness, our not-knowing-how-to-be rises up and overcomes it. So it is not without significance that we translate ourselves into comic book characters, doing our funny, futile dance across the desert. Incongruity is all we really understand.

I am getting very tired, worried that someone is going to get lost and be left behind in that endless maze of ravines. I begin to doubt that we will ever make it back; we will go on wandering forever among the rocks like the Israelites without a Moses. The longing for rest, for home, for a place to stay becomes physically acute, and I have to work hard on controlling my panic and anguish.

Strangely, no one gets lost, and soon we come up over the last hump that is the downward side of the irrigation canal. Walking along it single file, we smell the heavy night fragrance of the sacra datura bushes blooming there, the native psychedelic used in past ages by the Indians but alien to us. We tramp noisily across the wooden bridge and are home.

As we enter the glaring electric blaze of the house, the magic of the desert and the river clang down behind us. It is like passing a physical barrier.

The two children are caked with mud. One of them has gotten a cactus thorn in her foot. The chemical euphoria is gone, but the physical effects that become handicaps when something must be done remain. Assembling soap and water and towel, scrubbing away the mud, disinfecting the cut, are all tasks requiring great effort and concentration. The others have dumped the dirty dishes in the kitchen and disappeared into the dining room-library to talk off the rest of the chemicals. I feel angry and deserted. As I sit in the kitchen looking at the spills on the impossible concrete floor, feeling the food drying and caking in the dishes around me, the quintessence of the despair all housewives feel at the inevitable cyclical drudgery of their lives settles over me. The voices from the other room surge with laughter.

Finally the children are bathed and sent to bed. I creep out the sagging screen door and down the line of windows and doors to the large stone room I share with Jack. I know everyone else is sitting around the big oak table— *my* big oak table—eulogizing the day and themselves. How great it was to be in the midst of nature, to be really living, to be surrounded by such caring comrades. I know they are all lying, and I want them to realize it. To taste as bitterly as I do the deceit of their words. Not only the casual and literal dumping of their responsibility, but the lies they continue to tell themselves, their self-congratulation. Certainly they don't care about me. And how could they? They don't even know me. My depression and self-pity are gargantuan. Someone comes to the door and I growl at the figure to go away.

I want desperately to escape into sleep, but it will be hours before the motor that has become my mind will slow its racing enough for that. I pace back and forth. Sit and stare at the rough concrete wall that shapes and reshapes itself into maps of unknown worlds, each indentation a continental shelf.

I know, with one part of my mind, that this will end eventually. Yet with the part of me that feels time, it seems it will never end. I am caught in a time trap, a cage through whose bars I can look out and see tomorrow and myself released and in control again. But at this moment I cannot reach that freedom.

I cry and rage and hate until even that emotional pool is drained dry. And still all I can do is wait. Wait. Empty and dry and despairing. Separated not only from the desert, the rocks, the cottonwood tree, and the clouds, but from the human figures around me. My thoughts, I know, would be alien and shocking to them, still riding on that shimmering wave of optimism and good feeling. I am so weary and long for rest. Obliteration would be welcome. Simply to disappear into the dark night, dropping beyond memory, beyond time.

3

And I will put enmity between you and the woman, and between your offspring and her offspring; he shall crush your head and you shall snap at his heel.

—Genesis 3:15

To be brief, therefore, let the readers know, that they have then truly apprehended by faith what is meant by God being the Creator of heaven and earth, if they, in the first place, follow this universal rule, not to pass over, with ungrateful inattention or oblivion, those glorious perfections which God manifests in his creatures, and, secondly learn to make such an application to themselves as thoroughly to affect their hearts.

—Calvin, *Institutes*, I, xiv, 21

ob's cat, Rusty, was only one of our many pets, shadows of ourselves, almost like well-worn teddy bears that served whatever function the specific situation called for.

Different dogs ran under our feet at various stages of our history. There was Dina, a badly beaten and undernourished German shepherd someone had rescued, who licked everyone compulsively. Paris, a runt weimaraner, also neurotic, who fortunately disappeared several months after our arrival. Pucci, another foundling, short, curly and evil-tempered, lost in the streets of town. Phoebe

Zeitgeist, a kitten actually born at Moriah who was taken off by one of our emigrés. Her brother, Chef Boyardee, who, while exploring the roof one day, fell through the stovepipe opening to a gruesome death in the ashes below. And Jennifer, an adolescent Airedale of the latter era who refused to be housebroken.

None of these animals provided us with anything but a mirror. To confront animal life, I discover now, it is necessary to deal with something other than pets. We were the downfall of our dogs; whatever souls they had were distorted by contact with us.

Of course, there was no clear idea then of confronting a type of life different from our own to see what mysteries it would open to us. But in a hazy, suburban-starved way we knew animals were special, could tell us something. Thus many of us were eager to "get into animals," as we so clumsily put it, some because animal husbandry seemed more interesting than hoeing corn, some because it seemed more masculine, some from the desire to domesticate. Who knows all the reasons?

At any rate, our first animal acquisitions were, safely enough, rabbits. Lillian brought them out on the train all the way from Missouri. Four white, not quite grown rabbits. We hurried them home to the farm, put them in the dilapidated cages that our nameless precursor had used, opened our brand-new sack of rabbit pellets, filled the water dishes, and waited. The rabbits only stared back from their strange pink eyes. They would have been a lesson in passive resistance and guerrilla tactics had we had sense enough to observe that. As soon as we fed them and had had our fill of staring and left them alone, they immediately began chewing through the chicken wire, the wood frames, any destructible part of their cage.

It was a constant battle, keeping the rabbits in. We would go out to feed them in the mornings, only to find the entire herd furtively munching away the lettuce patch. An hour's chase ensued, the human predators trying to entrap the small darting figures before the dogs could fall upon them.

For every new litter of babies there was a corresponding new disease to keep the population stable. Our visions of a rabbit farm began to dim. Buying expensive feed, cutting alfalfa by hand, cleaning cages,

doing makeshift repairs on hutches. Twice a day attendance with the water pail. In this way the prey
wreaks revenge on the parasite.

And always the rabbits resisted us. One could count
on several long red scratches for each transfer of a rabbit from one cage to another—for mating, for kindling,
for the never-ending repairs. If we handled the babies,
we inevitably found the stiff little bodies on the ground
the next morning. Our rabbits had a strong sense of
ritual purity.

Once we began collecting rabbits, they seemed to
pour in from all our Chicano neighbors who must have
already recognized their folly. Thus our herd grew, not
so much from reproduction as from rejection.

Our suburban sensibilities disturbed by the incarcera-
tion of creatures in hutches, we finally tried making a
rabbit yard, fenced in with a shed for shelter, in order to
more closely approximate their natural habitat. We had
reckoned without their natural territorial imperatives,
however. The males fought ferociously and had to be put
back in isolation. The does and babies co-existed fairly
peaceably, but their escape instinct did not subside. The
hard red clay, like stone to our garden tools, yielded to
their sharp toenails like loam. Elaborate tunnels appeared overnight from the shed to the outside world.

Once, after our herd had been pretty well depleted
of breedable stock, I heard of a family in the next village who was selling its rabbits. Along with Simon, a
silversmith who'd joined our group, I loaded a refrig-
erator-size cardboard box on the back of the truck and
started off to find this bargain. A cold wind full of dirt
was whipping at the weak winter light as we bumped
along the back roads, trying to follow our sketchy di-

rections to the Villanuevas. Finally we ferreted out the right house and inquired at the door. The woman who answered listened to us stony-faced and then referred us without comment to her son who had just come home from school.

The Villanueva rabbit enterprise had deteriorated even more than ours. The boy had kept the rabbits for a 4-H project, now happily behind him. The rabbit reticence had almost gone out of these creatures. Instead of guerrillas, they were near to open combat with their keepers. Loose in even a larger pen than ours, they were only tossed occasional batches of hay and watered in rusty hubcaps. Their burrows in the sand were worthy of wild rabbits, and probably all that kept them from escape were the equally half-wild dogs that blinked at them from the other side of the fence.

The boy, with evident relief that this was his last bout with his adversaries, entered the cage and began throwing himself upon them with a rage that only springs from retribution. The rabbits scattered screaming. Gradually he closed in on each one, lunging after them, catching their hind legs and throwing them in high arcs, their long lean bodies struggling against the dirty wind, into the box on the truck bed.

When it was over, he brushed at the dirt that covered him, left the cage door hanging on its hinges in the wind, and accepted our money the way a conqueror accepts tribute.

After a year and a half of rabbit handling, the last few months of which were filled with stringy rabbit stews, the sole survivor of this experiment was a sickly white angora called Furball. His eyes were constantly infected; he had refused to breed with any of the does we tempted him with; he would even allow himself to be cuddled by the children. Lacking the requisite ruthlessness of real nomads, we carted Furball and his unwieldy cage around for three more moves after we left the farm, finally disposing of him in much the same manner he had been dumped on us.

Late in our first fall we decided to branch out into larger animals. Being politically averse to cows, which after all were responsible for the deplorably overgrazed condition of this part of the country, we decided on goats. All the homesteading books and magazines recommended these creatures as clean, intelligent, easily maintained, and productive.

Again Simon and I, in the pickup, started over the mountains to a retirement village a hundred miles away where, we had heard, some goats were for sale. The day was bright and beautiful, and the lush mountain meadows that flourished in what had once been volcanic craters filled our hearts with dreams—sleek, frisky creatures drowning us with their rich milk.

We reached the village, found our goat-lady, and began the long bargaining process. Many retirees in that part of the country, from the security of their pensions and odd jobs, doted on hippies, indeed, almost made them their hobby. Particularly the naturopathetically inclined who thrived on yeast and lecithin. In this woman's trailer were boxes containing tiny wheat farms in various stages of sprouting. She fed the wheat grass to her cats and munched handfuls herself. Outside were the remains of a garden truly to be proud of, with such exotics as Jerusalem artichokes, the roots of which she insisted upon digging up for us to plant in our own patch.

"Absolutely no trouble at all," she assured us. "Just stick 'em in the ground and next year you'll have these great big sunflower-type plants," she gestured the predicted height above her head, "and underneath these little yellow potato-like things." We gratefully accepted the free sample with visions of a full root cellar next year.

Everything the woman touched, eccentric and talkative as she was, seemed to thrive: her miniature indoor wheat farms, her garden, her apple trees, and most of all her goats. They behaved with admirable goat-like energy. She demonstrated the milk, which came in vigorous squirts into the plastic pail. We sampled and were sold. We took a full-grown white female of breedable age and a Nubian adolescent female ready to breed in six more months. Into the truck they went after many promises on our part to give them a good home and instructions on her part of what that entailed.

The drive home was somewhat less ideal than the morning trip had been. Weekend traffic out of Albuquerque piled up around us. The truck began to overheat and make strange noises. As darkness fell I developed fears of leading two strange goats down the highway in the cold with no hope of hitchhiking. We managed to limp home, though, and unload the frightened, indignant animals in the dark.

The next day began a more serious enslavement than the rabbits had ever required. They at least had been ostensibly passive; the goats were openly aggressive. Maisie, the older white one, never ever agreed with us about anything. During a week-long visit, she did manage to get impregnated by a billy belonging to friends who lived fifty miles away. And she did, in the course of time, bring forth two lovely golden kids who doubled the amount of time we spent mending the fence. But only in those ways did she follow the book. She did not produce the predicted gallons of milk. What we did squeeze out of her she generally managed to kick over, despite our attempts to follow the best milking techniques in the book.

Matilda was another matter. She was a picture-book goat, frisky and mischievous. She danced and cavorted, willful and unpredictable. But picturesqueness was about all she supplied. And as she became larger and stronger and her cavorting harder to control, her charms, like those of a precocious spoiled child, began to pale.

Still we kept the faith, milking twice a day, determined to strip the last drop from the recalcitrant teat, pouring over the 1931 Farm Bureau pamphlets, resolved to make it work, bewildered as to why it didn't. We read of success after success in *Mother Earth News* and *Organic Gardening* and grew more ashamed of our own failure.

The birth of the kids the next year offered some relief from our discouragement. We all sat hunkered in the goat stall or on top of the fence watching something actually happening. The quivering gelatinous balloons slowly emerged as Maisie panted and strained at her work, intent and oblivious to us. The delicate little hooves had never yet touched earth. The silky ears took shape before our eyes as the mother licked them clean. It was a miracle that they moved, that they were real. Finally something had turned out the way it should, the way it had been promised.

With four goats quartered near the garden, it was necessary to have them carefully watched during the day when they grazed. Jane, the youngest child and unburdened with school, got the job, not one she disliked, for of all of us, Jane was closest to the animals. She was still, in a way, one of them. She didn't hold their un-cooperativeness against them. She wasn't angry if Maisie kicked over the milk or a rabbit scratched her. She never expected the animals to be useful. They were simply companions, like people. I don't think it was out of sentimentality that I observed that they trusted her slightly more than the rest of us. After all, she never kicked them or cursed them and was impatient with us when we did.

But even Jane had trouble with the chickens. Like our other animals, they were secondhand, castoffs of the more experienced. Not realizing that we were buying a flock of hens past their prime, along with a nasty rooster, we unloaded our new experiment into their mite-ridden pen and waited for the eggs to come rolling in. And for about a month they did. We even marketed some. Then cold weather began to set in and the flow of eggs grad-ually diminished and finally stopped altogether.

Despite the elegant little societies of Hawthorne's and Hardy's fowl yards, I believe chickens invite indigni-ties. Their exaggerated fright at the most innocent movement or noise belied their confident strutting and scratching. Their squawking and shoving over food was much more offensive than the mute greed of the rab-bits and goats. In short, they were ridiculous creatures, puffed up and pompous over an insubstantial self-im-portance. Never did they try to escape, except as an un-organized group if the gate was left open. Above all they were stupid.

When we finally discovered, after poring over our agri-cultural manuals, that they must be vermin-infested, we took action, trapping them in the hen house and then one by one catching them in a flurry of feathers and squawks and incontinent droppings, stuffing them in a sack of sulphur dust, and giving them a sound shaking.

Late in the winter they suffered a more serious setback. Roving dogs broke into the pen while we were gone for the day and decimated their numbers. As we drove up in the twilight, we saw the dogs slinking off in the brush along the irrigation ditch, white feathers drooping for their guilty muzzles. Chickens littered the field around the pen, some still struggling against death. The survivors huddled in a traumatized pile in a corner of the hen house. I had never seen even rabbits so frightened. Rabbits would at least fight back. But the chickens were immobilized.

It was a miserable cleanup job. No one had been fond of the chickens, yet watching them suffer in this hopeless way was somehow different from shaking them in sulphur dust. We kept the half that remained, partly as a memorial to their martyred relatives, partly because we didn't know what else to do with them.

The rooster had survived the massacre, which did not add to our respect for him. We must have had some romantic notion of his defending his harem even to the death. He was not safe to turn your back on, had to be approached gingerly, was insanely jealous of the territory of the chicken pen. It was best to edge around the fence, dart quickly into the house, dip out the feed, and hope to distract him into eating while you tipped water into the troughs. Once he began to do his battle dance, there was nothing to do but grab a broomstick and hope to fend him off till you could get out the gate.

Bees were the only other creatures we kept for any length of time, and they were hardly in the animal class. For one thing they were totally independent of us. We neither fed nor watered them. The most caretaking we ever did on their behalf was to provide them with hives. Yet had they found themselves cramped for space, they would have simply taken up quarters elsewhere, a move we lived in perpetual fear of once the spring came. The time we spent scraping wax from frames, inspecting for queen cells and disease, extracting honey from the frames was solely for our own benefit and in no way contributed to the bees' well-being. If anything, it was a nuisance to them. In other words, we were completely the parasites in this situation, and if the arrangement turned out to be profitable in a small way, it was only because we had finally bought into a solvent corporation, one that had its collective head together, through no contribution of ours. Furthermore, in no way did they ever reflect anything about us; there was some inexplicable barrier that prevented any true intercourse between us.

We got our eleven hives of bees in the winter, perfect timing for once since bees are conveniently indoors during cold weather. We had to be up all night, loading and unloading them, because they can't see in the dark and very few will venture out. In all, the hives required about forty hours of maintenance that spring, and then the honey flow began. Unlike Maisie, they didn't have to be nudged into reluctant production. They did not constantly try to escape like the rabbits. They did not make stupid noises or go into witless hysteria like the chickens. If they were inclined to be somewhat cranky on cloudy, windy days, at least their emotionalism was not without cause.

The bees, above all, inspired respect. Hence the suit of armor one was obliged to put on before approaching them. One slip of the scraping knife, one dead bee, and you could count on being covered by a battalion of enraged black Italians, all ready to give their unreflective lives for the protection of the hive. Jack eventually reached the point where he could work with them uncovered, but cautiously. My own reaction to a bee attack, especially bees caught in my hair, was panic. There is something about the determination of a bee—relentlessly inhuman as only insects can be—that froze me with fear.

Still, it was that very inhumanness, that efficiency, that perfect programming that demanded our respect. If we had turned the other animals free, they could not have survived in an unprotected, unsubsidized environment for long. But the bees would not have missed our ministrations in the slightest. Yet they were by far the most productive for us, actually turning a small profit. The other animals we were forced to dispose of in one unsatisfactory way or another, but when we turned back to look at the farm for the last time, the beehives were still standing, humming in unattended activity.

Except for the bees, all our animals were our captives. But one pair we at least caught in a fair chase. They were the two Welsh ponies that wandered over the rocky plain to the north of us. Wilson, our absentee landlord, had vaguely mentioned that some ponies had been included in the purchase of this land. Therefore, we staked these two out as our legal, if unsuspecting, property.

It was late fall when we decided to round up the ponies, bring them into the corral, and train them to pull a plow for the spring planting. By this time Jerry was with us. He had had some years of experience as a cowboy on a large ranch in southern New Mexico and was fired up to bring these fat, vacationing animals into useful servitude for us. He persuaded the rest of us to buy some used collars and tack, which he spent the evenings mending while telling tales around the fire of his cowboy days. He was a good storyteller; we hoped he was a great pony-breaker.

We woke one cold, windy morning to Jerry's insistence that this was the day for horse-catching. He had been watching their movements carefully, and today they were down in a field not far from the house. So about four of us put on our coats, wrapped up our heads, and trailed off behind Jerry to surround the ponies.

It was not nearly as easy as Jerry had led us to believe. The field the horses were in had been plowed, which made running, for us anyway, difficult. The gates of all the fields were down, and the ponies had no trouble at all keeping a jump ahead of us. The wind whipped the raw dirt in our faces as we stumbled along, sometimes falling full length between the furrows.

After I got used to the situation's being hopeless, the chase became the most fun I'd had since childhood. Indeed that's what it was like, running, whooping, and flailing our arms in the wind, trying to frighten the ponies into the ambush Jerry had prepared for them. We were soon breathless and panting from running, falling, and laughing. Still we ran, following Jerry's shouted instructions to bar the gate, get them in the corner, not let them through. Up the bare hills and down into the steep arroyos where junipers and cottonwoods provided cover. Now and then catching sight of a spotted side as it dashed to safety again.

The chase went on for hours and seemed to have no point anymore—just the running, the wind, the falling, the laughing—when Jerry suddenly shouted to us from the bottom of a rocky slope. He had them cornered against the angle of a fence down by the river. We rushed and slid down the rocky hill, serious again about our purpose.

While we kept the ponies from escaping, Jerry hurriedly roped off a makeshift corral to keep them penned in. The ponies, meanwhile, snorted and stamped at the far end of the fence, sending up sprays of river water as they danced impatiently.

Jerry slipped into the enclosure with them and began talking to them low and beguilingly. They weren't having any of it and pranced away, insulted.

It was like a dream by now. A long, drawn-out, slow-motion dream dance. Jerry advancing, horses retreating. Around and around. We were in a strange, beautiful world, the wind and the water whirling around us, the light falling into the arroyo illuminating a dream of chase, battle, entreaty. I wished it could have gone on forever. The wild, rolling eyes of the ponies watched Jerry crooning to them. At last he slipped a rope halter around the neck of one and then the other. Once the rope was on, they stood surprisingly docile.

It was afternoon by the time we led them, plodding and balky, back up the rocks, over the fields, and into the corral.

For a week Jerry worked with the ponies, leading them round and round the corral. It would be a long time, he admitted, before he could get them to work together in harness. As it turned out, he never had the opportunity to try.

One afternoon Sally discovered Suarez, our nearest neighbor, leading the two ponies by the ropes out of the corral and across the road toward his own pasture.

"Jerry," she called, "Jack. Come quick. Something's wrong."

Something was indeed wrong from Suarez's point of view. When Jerry and Jack accosted him in the road, he was ready with a tongue-lashing of which only a few words were in English, but enough of them for us to get the general drift of his sentiments. The ponies, he claimed, were his. They never had been Wilson's. If Wilson had any ponies of his own, let him produce them. And furthermore, we were not to impose on his hospitality any further. He had no truck with horse thieves. He had been looking for these ponies for a week now and had even alerted the sheriff to their disappearance. We were lucky we weren't all in jail.

Although the circumstances of their departure were unpleasant, I was almost relieved to see the ponies go. They ate tremendous quantities of hay, and Jerry had told us that when we started working them they would have to get grain. Besides, I never really believed the two stubborn beasts could be trained to the plow. We had already had the best part of them—the chase.

Taken all together, the animals gave me something deeper and more pervasive than "learning." They became a strata, a vein, in what was me. My worldview, my *blik*, as the philosopher R. M. Hare would say, now has in it the darting rabbit eyes staring at me, without recognition or trust, from a hollow in the hay. The weak, watery eyes of Furball I discount. His passivity was not trust. He had simply given up his rabbit spirit through some congenital defect, and though we pitied him (and thus did not eat him), our caretaking was only a token of our guilt.

For this paradox of guilt and necessity weighed down upon us every time Jack laid the lead pipe to the cortex of a palpitating rabbit body and nailed its hind legs to the shed wall to skin it. Thoreau went to the woods to live life close to the bone and suck its marrow. Christ starved in the wilderness to be tempted. But we found ourselves shivering at the sight of the bloody reality that confronted us on the shed wall. It's easy enough to be an optimistic pantheist when one is growing beans. But when you are imprisoning and killing an animal whose heart beats faster than your own, without even a fair chase, when you have to beat the innocent dogs away from the blood coagulating in the sand, when you know that given even four days without food you would be willing to eat the dogs themselves, and in forty days one another, you begin to touch the uneven outer limits of your possibilities.

I have eaten *cabrito* on a holiday in Mexico and know the delicious, crusty, sweet taste of kid's milk-fed flesh. I could sink my carnivore's teeth into it tomorrow with relish. But when one stands watching two ivory-colored kids butting one another in play and weighs whether this sight is more important than the sweet taste of their flesh, the ominous question of how we got this way begins to form on the horizon of the mind, a cloud no bigger than a man's hand.

And once we begin we are well into it. So you are suddenly swamped with vegetarian guilt while your hutch is full of rabbits. Do you expiate your own guilt by loosing them to their natural predators? Do you at the least demand that they stop breeding? Do you clear-headedly assess the lifestyle of aboriginal hunters and gatherers who take their "fair" place in the quest for food? Usually you hustle them off for someone else to worry over or you live with your guilt and meat.

However, becoming a vegetarian does not resolve the dilemma. Chickens, eggs; goats, milk. And the finer points of the law. The rabbits could smell the original sin on us. And if the goats knew on which side their bread was buttered, they also knew enough not to be grateful. If the chickens were hysterical, was it not with stir-craziness? Yet how do we live without premeditated exploitation? Unless we live as saints, facing early ex-termination, or as animals. There seems no simply human way to live, except in the dark crack between guilt and necessity.

Perhaps in this we are closer to the insects than we admit. The ants who keep herds of aphids. Larvae feed-ing on the living body of their host. We have a horror of and a fascination for the bees' efficiency. They do not stop at hounding useless males from the pack; they dispatch them at the door. There are no disobedient bees, no social deviants. Even their dancing is not, like the kids', from sheer exuberance of well-being or for fun, but to locate for the community new nectar fields.

But in the end we sneer at the hive society. We se-cretly cheer (while cursing) the ones who know we are not to be trusted, who acquiesce to no coexistence treaty with us, who never give up their attempts at escape. If we were an exploited animal, that is how we would hope to behave, and not like the poor stupid, addled chickens or the exhausted Furball. Whenever I heard that defiant thump of a rabbit's hind leg, something in my dark insides laughed exultantly: Don't give up, my little enemy. Your senses tell you right—I'm trying to kill you. Resist, resist your death, resist me. For as long as you resist, I know you are real. The world is real and not just a reflection of myself. And whatever it is in me that makes it necessary for me to kill you is being resisted and has not yet swallowed the whole, real world.

4

To the woman he said, "I shall greatly increase your pain and your pregnancy. In pain you shall bear children and yet you shall long for your husband. And he shall dominate you."

—Genesis 3:16

Men have died and worms have eaten them, but not for love.

—Shakespeare, *Romeo and Juliet*

Packed in among the dishes, the furniture, and the tools we brought with us to New Mexico were certain old patterns we had hoped to leave behind, and were in fact sure we had, until we began to try to live our new life. Then we discovered, rumpled but familiar, the same stale attitudes and ways of seeing one another we thought we had abandoned with our jobs, schools, and American society.

The first of these to come to light was the tension between the men and women. Communes have always been suspected of harboring indiscriminate, licentious sexuality.

Real life can't sustain such a fantasy for long, however. What we desired was innocence, not debauchery. But when a collection of people, all with very different backgrounds, expectations, and ways of being pleased, come together to live for an extended period, sexual fantasy deflates from a hundred different pressures.

Naturally, our attempts at defining and regaining the innocence we craved were sad little scenarios, but illumined now and again by some small hint of rightness that kept us struggling, never very successfully, toward our obscure vision. Two or three people, sunning naked on the rocks like soft, vulnerable lizards, could feel like contented children. But when we discovered that our supposedly secure outdoor shower was being lecherously observed by our neighbors, we were indignant.

Everyone craved an innocent sexuality, but nowhere could we find a pattern for it. Animals certainly provided no very happy model. Cats yowling in desperation; strange dogs invading our house when one of ours was in heat; the ferocious couplings of our rabbits when, as often as not, either the buck or the doe would be torn and bleeding after the encounter; the strutting cock in the chicken yard; the smelly billy we took our Maisie to for "servicing"; the dead drones strewn outside the hives after the pleasureless attacks of the workers—none of these appealed to us, although we could see their reflections in our own relationships. We did not despise the necessity that seemed to drive the animals we lived with; we only knew that human sexuality must mean something more.

Not that there wasn't a certain amount of prowling instinct inhabiting some of our hearts. The unattached people particularly felt their lot to be more than a little difficult, having come to this barren New Mexico farm thirty-five miles from the nearest town. No wonder that as the summer ripened more and more of them hitchhiked to Santa Fe for the weekend.

But for those who came with some relationship already formed or who developed one afterwards, matters were little better. In fact, in this stark setting, problems seemed to be magnified to almost unbearable proportions. For example, Don and Janet had been living together for at least a year before we came to New Mexico. Previously they had lived in a campus commune, pursuing a life of what news magazines commonly called radical activism—the vegetarian Food Conspiracy, women's liberation, the peace movement, free schools. Yet their relationship had all the dreary clichés of any middle-class marriage.

Janet was a tall, full-blown blonde, with the face and abundant hair of a Renaissance Venus. Protective and motherly, she was one of the few women who took enough interest in the two children to read to them, sew for them, or teach them anything new. Yet she was just as protective and motherly towards Don. Every morning she would get up and fix his breakfast separately from everyone else's because he liked to sleep late and didn't take well to boiled wheat or oatmeal. When some of the group began to protest, she defended this as Don's peculiar eccentricity, a mark of his personal freedom.

"Can't you even see what you're doing?" Sally would tell her. "For all your big ideas about being liberated, you're nothing more than a slave to Don's every whim."

Don himself came from a wealthy suburban family with a caricature cutthroat businessman for a father. He never tired of telling how his father had made him a standing offer of $1000 to cut his hair, which he had heroically turned down. As time wore on and the story thin, we all began to wish Don had been a little less principled and a lot more practical. Almost the sole content of Don's work was the rebuilding of his Harley Davidson motorcycle, which had broken down right after getting him and Janet to New Mexico. He had a real aversion to animals and gardening and threatened, like a petulant child, not to take his turn at dishwashing if people weren't more respectful of his freedom. Yet as long as his demands were gratified, he was good-natured and agreeable.

His dark handsomeness was a perfect foil to Janet's fairness. But their dependencies fitted together in a much more sinister way. Don was essentially Janet's child. She protected him from our attacks, coddled him, acceded to his wishes, was at the bottom of her heart afraid of losing him. He laughed at her nagging the way a confident, spoiled child will laugh at its mother, but deepened his dependence on her daily. Emotionally, they were incestuous.

It was not pleasant for the rest of us to watch this being acted out. First, it was all too typical of the homes some of us had come out of: the demanding father, the acquiescing mother, the nagging, the cruelty, the fear of losing love. We already knew that what we wanted was something different from this. Yet it had followed us, like an unlaid ghost, in the form of two people who intellectually knew better, who had read all the right books and belonged to the right groups but were powerless to change their behavior.

Moreover, there was a great gulf between Janet and the other women, who saw her as their betrayer. She was not playing fair; she was only managing to hold Don by satisfying his childish whims, and since several of them found Don remarkably attractive, they thought this rigged the competition. The others were simply enraged at the sight of a woman, a sister, prostrating herself so servilely and thus disgracing their sex.

On the other hand, Don had only superficial friendships with the men, since his childishness was resented or envied or both. They felt toward him as the older children often feel toward the baby of a family who is granted privileges they never had. Thus both Don and Janet were isolated from other friendships in the group and forced to rely all the more on each other, wearing the ruts of their relationship ever deeper.

———

Wayne and Faye had known one another only a few weeks before coming to New Mexico. Yet Wayne had quickly conceived one of those dark, brooding passions for Faye, who, unfortunately for him, did not reciprocate. At first she had found it convenient enough to have a handy partner, someone to talk and joke and sleep with. But soon she began feeling crowded, especially when Wayne suggested that they fix up one of the outbuildings for just the two of them. She was not all *that* committed, nor was she prepared to cut off whatever other possibilities might arise. She was out to seek her fortune, and Wayne, though fun enough in his own way, was no treasure.

Wayne was overwhelmed at this news. In his eyes Faye encompassed every quality he could ever wish for in a woman, and to be denied his heart's desire at this early stage made life a bleak prospect indeed. Faye suffered only minor twinges of guilt at disappointing him, but Wayne withdrew from the rest of human society to grieve with a vengeance. He proceeded with his plans to fix up one of the buildings and moved in alone. Of course, he never really gave up. He continued to entreat Faye to join him, and she continued to refuse, at first gently and later with annoyance.

The women, for the most part, treated Wayne's morose lovesickness with ridicule. For one thing it was morally wrong for him to try to force Faye into an arrangement against her will. The men, although they didn't really much care one way or another, still felt a trifle uneasy about the situation and were not quite so inclined to laugh at Wayne's sulks. Whether out of a fearful secret knowledge through which they could see themselves in his position or just a greater respect for Wayne's feelings, they would frown at the women's giggling at his departing back as he disappeared after each meal down the path to his hovel, his hands jammed into his jeans pockets and his head down.

Faye, for her part, was discreet but indiscriminate, keeping one eye on Don and one on every new male visitor. She played her flute in the summer evenings, was careful to achieve just the right kind of clever antiqueness with her clothes, tried seriously but unsuccessfully to accept her share of the work and responsibility, was generous with her resources. But everyone was made uneasy by her restlessness, her prowling search for a man. And although her friendships with other women were more solid than Janet's, they didn't trust her to respect any of their established relationships with the men.

Eventually Faye did find someone, at least temporarily. In the next village, where we got our mail, lived two brothers, raunchy types who had accrued enough money working in the Detroit car factories to buy their own land. Their parents were Russian immigrants and their life had been hard, unsoftened by even those meager consolations the middle class offers its children. They were strong, hard workers whenever they were not drunk or high, and usually good-natured when they were, although something dangerous lurked then too. Joe, the younger brother, had been on heroin for a while and still played around with it from time to time. Our community was friendly with them, but hesitant to be too neighborly, the usual reaction of protected radical theoreticians when they confront the raw, unmanageable material of their theories.

Faye, however, finding some glamorous allure in Joe's strange background, had at last found someone with a recklessness to match her own. His idea of a good time was walking as close to the edge of disaster as possible, which suited Faye's own propensities for pushing life to the extremes. So when Joe's brother went back to Michigan in the fall to make another bundle on the assembly line, Faye moved in with Joe.

We still saw Faye occasionally, of course. And while several of us were a little huffy about her leaving, we were also relieved at not having to worry anymore about *when* she would do it.

Faye did not fare so well, however. For the first couple of weeks she was romantically enthusiastic about the arrangement. She and Joe lived in an old one-room adobe shack on his property. She ordered the tiny house to her satisfaction, helped haul water from the village well, learned the peculiarities of the wood stove. Then the clashes began. While she had found Joe's rough offhandedness immensely satisfying to her sexual prototype of masculinity, when that same attitude got up out of the bed—or rather demanded that she get up out of the bed and fix his breakfast—or even when it demanded her attendance in bed when she didn't feel like it, the picture began to pale. She had always been a fierce liberationist, valuing her own freedom. But Joe, who had known only a much mistreated mother and sisters who had been taken advantage of at an early age, hadn't the least inkling of Faye's desires for respect and independence and didn't much care to learn. His life had always been catch-as-catch-can and devil-take-the-hindmost, and since he had survived so far, no mean task, he saw no reason to change for some soft-headed woman.

Faye learned the cost of evading the raucous demands not only of Joe, but of the drunken buddies he brought home. And by the time she found herself being knocked around for not obeying, the glamour had worn as thin as her patience. She packed up her belongings, paid us a farewell visit, and hitched further west, still looking for that El Dorado that contained both the Marlboro Man and Henry David Thoreau.

———

Unrequited love was as abundant in our midst as it is in folk songs. First there was Faye and Wayne, then later Lillian and Jerry. Lillian joined us in New Mexico immediately after she had obtained a very unsatisfactory divorce back in the Midwest. Not that there were any children involved or even any complicated property settlements. In fact, the divorce was not contested in any way. Her husband, an anthropologist, had simply left her, without a word of explanation, after six years of marriage. The unresolved rejection rankled in Lillian's neat, tidy soul, and she decided to redo herself entirely. She cut off her long hair, bought new clothes, quit her high-salaried job, and set out to seek her fortune. Her first stop was with us.

She arrived on the train with the four white rabbits, ready to set up an efficient, productive rabbit ranch. But even Lillian's bustling efficiency broke down before the massive, amorphous unwieldiness of destiny in the desert. Yet, much that did get done was owing to her. She repaired rabbit hutches, saw to their care, made herself a private room in the attic that no one had bothered with, canned tomatoes, and dried apples.

Jerry didn't join us till the fall. He came out of much the same sort of rough-and-ready background as Joe, but being a voracious reader, had been pollinated with the ideas in the air about new lifestyles. Extremely clever at making things, Jerry was much more interested in the pragmatics of such ideas—developing a methane power plant, a wind generator, solar-heated buildings—than in new human relationships. In fact, he joined us right after having been released from the state mental hospital where he had been incarcerated for beating up his mother.

A tall, lanky cowboy, he was as strong and willing as they come, painfully eager for human company that would accept him and appreciate his worth. He was also a great storyteller, having the kind of checkered past that makes for endless tales. He was immediately a great favorite of everyone.

It didn't take him long to single out Lillian. She had grit, determination, resourcefulness—all characteristics he valued highly. And besides, she was small and pretty, even dainty, which intrigued him. But Lillian was having none of it. Although she felt sisterly affection for Jerry, he was not at all her sort. She made none of the impetuous mistakes that Faye had, yet the situation was no better. Jerry was as hopelessly infatuated with her as Wayne had been with Faye.

Jerry had been honest with us about his background. He had even showed us the anti-depressant medication that had been prescribed for him in the hospital. But he had proved himself to be so easygoing and agreeable that we had finally chalked it all up to another great blunder by the forces of Society. After Lillian rejected him (that took a while to sink in), however, he began a tailspin into the outer reaches of depression. At first he was only gloomy and uncommunicative. When this had no effect on Lillian, he withdrew even deeper into his own special darkness. He would no longer go outdoors and work, then he wouldn't even leave his room, and finally he took to his bed.

The rest of us were simply bewildered by this behavior. Lillian of course refused to give in or to offer him any false hope. She was just as offended by this undisguised emotional blackmail as Faye had been. Yet we couldn't simply shrug and smile wryly at Jerry the way we had with Wayne. Wayne had isolated himself and been touchy and tender, until eventually he had packed up his broken heart and left. But Jerry was a more drastic case. The deeper his depression grew, the more dangerous he became. We urged him to take his medication, but he refused. If he was going to suffer, so were we all. And it was obvious he was spoiling for a fight, someone on whom to vent his frustrated feelings.

One winter morning, without a word to anyone, he began packing all his belongings, making a clatter and fuss so that we all got the message that he intended to leave. Lillian was elated and joked nervously in the kitchen with Sally about her large, lumbering Lothario who was finally giving up. All of us had learned not to ask Jerry any questions, since we got either no answers or very unsatisfactory ones. We watched his packing furtively.

When I saw him stalk off to the bathhouse to retrieve his things, I felt a sudden pang of remorse. Perhaps we hadn't done all we might to make things easier for Jerry. In his crumpled cowboy hat and torn jacket he looked destitute of all human friendship. I could approach him more easily than anyone else; my matron's status seemed to hold some special significance for him. So I followed him down to the bathhouse, determined to talk.

It was a grey, dreary day. Inside the dank building musty hay and cornstalks were piled in the corner, harboring mice and spiders. We sat on the side of the bathtub to talk and propped our feet on the blackened wood stove where we heated the bath water.

I began in my gentlest voice, hoping to appeal to Jerry's idea of the feminine. Still, I never knew at what moment I might tread on some territory mined with terrible memories and associations.

"Are you leaving, Jerry?"

A long pause. "Yep."

"Why? We don't want you to." Not exactly true, but it *could* have been under other conditions.

"She does."

"You mean Lillian?"

He ignored my question and reflected on his own assertion. "She'll be happier when I'm not around. It's either her or me. I can't stand it any longer."

"But you're both important to us, Jerry. We need you as much as her." True enough, but a not quite fair way of putting it. And totally ignoring the fact that Lillian would never leave on Jerry's account.

"That may be, but I've got to get out of here. I thought when I first came here that this was really heaven, that I'd found what I'd been looking for all my life. But I got fooled again, and I've got to move on. I appreciate what you and Jack and everyone has done for me, but it's just not working out."

"But Lillian's not the only fish in the pond," I protested. "You can't let something like this spoil all your plans." The look on his face warned me not to push this any further. I hadn't taken his pain seriously enough.

"Well," he said gruffly, standing up to leave, "I know when I've got to leave. Thanks for everything."

"Good-bye, Jerry. There'll be a place for you whenever you want to come back." I stood up and gave him a farewell peck on the cheek.

Perhaps he felt a small bit better that someone had broken through his own stubborn silence and at least said good-bye properly. But it was no more than a Band-Aid on a festering wound. There was no healing and no desire for healing. Jerry's disease had become his identity.

Jack offered to take him out to the highway where he could hitchhike to Santa Fe. He climbed in the back of the truck and sat on the wheel well, balancing his duffle bag between his knees and not looking back.

———

Sally had joined us in New Mexico carefree and un-attached. She was one of those rare eager-hearted people ready to love almost anyone on a moment's notice. When her art teacher had assigned her the project of designing restaurant chairs so uncomfortable that no one would linger more than thirty minutes, she had dropped out of art school in a moral huff. Now she had ambitions of becoming a weaver, if she could ever find some place to set up a loom.

The first summer she spent shuttling back and forth between Moriah and Santa Fe, trying to find a job, trying to find a spot, trying to find what she called an "ogle man." She was small and svelte, full of high spirits and daring, and almost everyone's darling, especially the children's, among whom she really counted herself. She could make up funny songs and games on long afternoons, put together elaborate costumes for them, and generally make our hard times appear a lark.

But the more Sally brightened, the more shadows seemed to hedge her in. Her family history had some large dark spots. And the friends she made so easily and gave herself to so freely were not always as loyal and loving in return.

As fall came on and the handful of short-lived jobs she had held during the tourist season in Santa Fe dried up, she came back to the farm to settle in for the winter. Meanwhile, we had added another new member, Simon, the silversmith and a college drop-out. In contrast to Sally, Simon was solemn, slow, and liked to meditate a lot. Once in a while a ripple of humor or anger would cross the otherwise placid surface of his psyche, but mostly he worked at being as inscrutable as a Buddha.

None of us could ever understand what drew the two of them together to begin with. True, almost anyone was instantly attracted to Sally, but then she was much more vivacious and open than Simon seemed to think suitable for the properly spiritual life. On the other hand, skinny Simon with only his golden wavy hair, of which he was secretly vain, to recommend him physically, did not at all seem the sort Sally would take as a lover. He was no "ogle man" to be sure and scorned levity. There were times though when I think he was hungry for it and longed to join in, only he didn't know how and was afraid of looking ridiculous. So we stood by and watched the liaison develop, not wanting to put our oar in where it wasn't wanted, but expecting no good to come from it. And of course we weren't disappointed.

The two of them soon decided to move into the same outbuilding that the ill-fated Wayne had fixed up for Faye. The farmhouse was depressing enough, but that place was even worse. Directly below the irrigation canal, it was always damp and moldy. With only one small window, and that one facing north, it was also dark. The floor was dirt, but Wayne had plastered the walls inside, which at least slowed the crumbling process. There was, of course, no water or heat. As winter began to set in, these inauspicious surroundings would have put a strain on all but the hardiest of alliances. And everything Simon undertook was merely speculative, never hardy.

Soon Sally grew unnaturally morose. At first she was reluctant to talk about her situation, feeling it would be disloyal to talk about Simon behind his back. But finally she admitted to Lillian and me that she was utterly miserable. Simon wanted affection with half his heart, but pushed it away with the other half. Touching and kissing and laughing were painful to him. He wanted Sally to be more serious, meaning more respectful of his self-consciously ascetic ways. Still she felt enough good things were buried in him to make the effort worthwhile. Yet she was freezing to death inside and out.

They never fought, of course. Pacifistic Simon would have died rather than openly shout at someone. It was silence, silence and cold and pretense that stifled them. He wanted affection and warmth but was ashamed of wanting it and consequently told himself, and Sally, that it was superior not to want it. And Sally, having made a commitment to Simon out of who knows what sort of desperation, hung on, refusing to admit the defeat of her desire to love and be loved by someone. Yet she weakened every day and grew more tearful.

Mercifully, it ended at last with her illness. She needed an operation, which took her away to Denver for a month. Simon, of course, never gave a sign that her going altered anything in his life. He was solicitous in a distant way about her health. But if there was any hole left in his life by her absence, he never let anyone know.

When she came back, she and Simon did not take up their old relationship. They were stiffly friendly but that was all. If they reached any other kind of resolution, we never knew about it. Sally's desperate search continued, and Simon grew more confirmed in his detachment.

Not long after this, Sally, Lillian, and I were staying at a friend's apartment in town recuperating from a newly diagnosed case of paratyphoid. We were enjoying the easy warmth of the furnace heat, the relatively clean surroundings, a flush toilet, and hot water. In this cozy atmosphere we waxed philosophical about relationships between men and women, a subject that often preoccupied us.

"I don't think that I will ever again have a permanent relationship with any man," Lillian said. "It's too much hassle for too little reward."

"But I can't live without men," protested Sally. "It's no fun."

"Well," said Lillian in her most no-nonsense tone, "that doesn't have to mean anything permanent. Why do we have to hurt and hurt just for someone to sleep with and a chuck under the chin once in a while? From now on for me it's only going to be transient affairs." She savored the last two words as only a resolute apostate from respectability can.

"Transient affairs," Sally agreed. And though at the time it truly seemed like the most sensible solution in the world, a way of cutting your losses while at least not decreasing the rewards, I know neither of them has strictly stuck to her plan.

———

These are all stories of people bound by no legal or familial ties, people trying on and discarding, with some facsimile of freedom, various sorts of relationships. But what of Jack and me who had been married ten years and had two daughters?

Before we came here, our marriage had become a painful, comfortable trap, padded with plastic apartments, several degrees, teaching positions, and Bankamericards. Somehow those youthful pictures we had carried around inside us for years, plans of what we were going to do with our precious lives, were aborting, dying without ever having seen the light of day. We had been to Europe and Mexico, bought a camper and spent nights on the Gulf Coast beach, a vacation in the Rockies, and a summer in Taos. But these were only sops for the excitement we longed for.

On one particular day distinct in my memory, we were sitting around our dinner table with our daughters, watching the heat turn the asphalt to black bubbles and the newly planted tree outside our apartment window drooping in the blasting sun, when the despairing thought flashed through my brain that life would never be any different than this, that we were caught. There was no way out.

My notion of the trap at that time was primarily economic. We couldn't afford to give up our jobs and explore the world. We had two children to support. It was not until these dissatisfactions became irrational resentments against one another and each of us began to see the other as a part of our own trap that we were forced to find a way out. Even an animal, if it is desperate enough, will gnaw off its own leg to escape the trap. And in our desperate state we went about gnawing at one another.

Not that our goals were at variance, although they were rather amorphous and vague. We both wanted something we called freedom: freedom from the kinds of time limitations ordinary jobs demanded, freedom from meaningless conventions and conformity, freedom from an "unnatural," hemmed-in life. But most of all, freedom from emptiness.

I remember the long, empty, bored Sunday afternoons straight out of *The Waste Land.* "What shall we do, what shall we ever do?" Go see equally bored friends, get up a party, drive out into the country. The Sunday paper scattered around the living room, the girls cross and fidgety, a dull, cottony taste in the mouth. We grew as quarrelsome as children shut up indoors on a perpetual rainy day.

Yet there were still moments when we shared our gropings after something more, the ineffable "more," more than this dead-end, pointless life. And these moments kept us knit together, however tenuously.

We tried separate households for a year. We were 250 miles apart, but one or the other of us commuted almost every weekend. As the experiment developed, however, I was even less satisfied than before. I had the children and a full-time job. Although I said this was what I wanted, a chance to earn my own living, stand on my own two feet, I was dreadfully lonely. I had gnawed off my leg and escaped from the trap, but found myself only ambiguously free and definitely crippled.

Jack, meanwhile, had found an exciting new role to play. Having been married since our freshman year in college, he had never known anything but the constant economic imperative of provide, provide. Now he was able to loosen up, grow grungy, get inflamed with radical politics. He had a bachelor apartment with a friend and lived the free and easy life of a graduate student.

It was during this year that we formulated our plans for New Mexico. We had wiggled loose enough from the structures that bound us to begin to see a way out. I was ready to move on, and Jack, although his life was more appealing than it had been, was becoming increasingly alienated from competitive academic degree-gathering. His participation in the campus strike that spring was the deathblow to his teaching aspirations.

Our need for one another was still compulsive. After ten years of changes, each had become a repository of the other's history. No one else in the whole world knew us as well as we knew each other. We relied on one another to know who we were; if we were cut off from one another, we would also be cut off from our own identities, our own selves. But at the same time, it is not always pleasant to be reminded of who you are, accused of your identity. There were times when we wanted to smash the mirror staring us in the face.

Jack, for instance, was such a conflicting bundle of impulses that it was almost impossible for him to act except out of frustration with those conflicts. No one's soul ever burned with a whiter flame against social injustices than Jack's. He could have made a great crusader or guerrilla, and perhaps would have had he not been encumbered by a family. Yet at the same time, he had grown up in a lower middle-class home and had built into him all those aspirations for comfort, for easy movement, for conspicuous signs of success. To walk into a bank now and be hassled because his clothes and hair were not respectable filled him with both indignation and shame. And the frustration of not being able to reconcile these two conflicting emotions often exploded into irrational anger.

He demanded a very high standard of conduct from the other people at Moriah—loyalty, hard work, unselfishness, order—nothing less than he expected from himself. But when these expectations collided with the prevailing tenet of counterculture faith, namely, that it is wrong to make demands on anyone, that personal freedom is the highest good, the combustion caused by the friction between the two ideas brought down fire on everyone's heads.

Jack in a rage was terrible to behold, a cross between Jeremiah and Rasputin. His nuclear family had borne the brunt of his frustrations with academia and his clinging to its security. Now his extended family was catching it because our ideological illusion of freedom conflicted with the need for strict discipline to survive at Moriah. Intimidated by his thunderous assaults, the weaker ones were scared away by the end of the first summer.

My own unconfessed intention had been to gather other people about us to dilute the intensity of our private partnership. I wanted to form an alliance against Jack, to throw up a barricade of unsuspecting bodies between us. Other people, I was convinced, would sympathize and take my part against this tyrant. Eventually there would be others who knew me as well as Jack did and who, of course, would love me. Then I would be free! I wouldn't need Jack anymore. He, I thought with secret vengeance, could go choke on his own anger and disappointments. For my part, I would have built up a backlog of friends who recognized my worth. I would never need to be lonely again.

Our motives, then, were the darkest and most devious of all, sometimes hidden even from ourselves. While everyone else's purposes were not always in line with the revolutionary rhetoric they espoused, at least they were usually transparent. But in our private battle, all others were merely weapons we used against each other.

Of course, we were not quite so skilled at manipulation as we supposed. Life resisted us too firmly. Our extended family, each person with his or her own personal goals, outmaneuvered us continually. And in the end, instead of the lines being drawn between my side and Jack's, we found ourselves back on the same side of the barricades, us against them.

This in itself was unhealthy. We were not really able to take seriously other people's needs. Our first demand was that they sacrifice all their private dreams to ours—the success of the commune at Moriah. Then they could go on with their lives with their leftover time and energy. Every time someone left, we tried to appear understanding. But in our hearts we scorned them as failures. These desertions, as we saw them, drove us up against the wall together. We learned, once and for all, the meaning of "forsaking all others."

This didn't put an end to our terrible fights, but at least more mutual territory was marked out now that we no longer deluded ourselves with dreams of a diluted marriage. I remember one particularly hot, dusty day after an explosive parting with one of our original group. We quarreled over Jack's overly generous offer to stock the deserter up with food and take him the thirty miles down to the main highway where the chances of hitching were better.

"Gas costs money," I complained. "And he's freeloaded long enough. If he's so anxious to do his own thing, let it be his *own* thing."

Jack was suddenly furious, more enraged than I had seen him in months.

"You can't talk that way," he yelled, throwing his keys across the room. He pushed me aside and stormed out the bedroom door, slamming it behind him. I followed, aghast at what was happening, sure that if ever we needed to stick together against the rest of the world it was now, when everyone else was deserting us. In the living room he was crying, great heaving sobs, and pounding his fists into the plaster. I was crying and beseeching him to tell me what was the matter.

"You," he screamed, "you and your stupid, grasping, tight-fistedness." He paused, and for a moment I held back all the justifications, all the instances of my own overtaxed generosity. And that moment of restraint was a gift of grace. Instead of the argument degenerating into the usual recriminations against one another's failures, it gave him the chance to say: "I don't care. I don't care if people take advantage of me or if I give away more than they 'deserve.' If I can't do that, if I can't, once in a while, be magnanimous, then I don't care about living this life. It doesn't mean anything if it's only fighting and grasping and holding off the rest of the world. If that's what life is, I don't want it, I don't want it."

I caught my breath as the words came out of his mouth. He was right, he was right. To always be cringing in a corner and afraid of advantages being taken, to be always in the protective position—even if we lost everything (and heaven knows we had little enough to lose then)—it wasn't worth even life itself. Whatever other secondary goals we had—a homestead of our own, a free life, whatever—there was something more essential to both of us than that, and without it we would die from a dream gone sour.

It was only the beginning of clarity, of course. It was to be a while longer before we could formulate

86

any better what was at the bottom of both of us that kept us together. But it was a true beginning, and it was fortunate that it happened then because, although we didn't know it, we were just entering a chapter of our story that would be more difficult and bitter than anything we had known before.

5

Cursed is the ground because of you. In grief you shall eat of it all the days of your life. Thorns and thistles shall spring up for you and you shall eat the plants of the field. With the sweat of your face you shall eat bread until you return to the ground.

—Genesis 3:17–19

*a flower within a flower whose history
(within the mind) crouching
among the ferny rocks, laughs at the names
by which they think to trap it. Escapes! Never by
running but by lying still*

—William Carlos Williams, *Paterson*

f a dark gulf filled with ancient enmity lay between us and the animals, an even deeper, more impenetrable mystery infused the land. This was not the familiar, rich, domesticated farmland of the Midwest, leveled, parceled, and calculable. It was rugged open range where the few fences were built to keep stock out, not in.

According to old reports, the ground had been covered with range grasses that were belly-high on the horses of the Spanish settlers. Don Juan Oñate, entering for the first time what is now New Mexico, wrote to the Viceroy, the Count of Monterey, on March 2, 1659:

It is a land abounding in flesh of buffalo, goats with hideous horns, and turkeys. . . . There are many wild and ferocious beasts, lions, bears, wolves, tigers, penicas, ferrets, porcupines, and other animals whose hides they tan and use. Towards the west there are bees and very white honey, of which I am sending a sample. Besides, there are vegetables, a great abundance of the best and greatest salines in the world, and a very great many kinds of very rich ores, as I stated above.

Now only the thinnest tussocks of buffalo grass grew sparsely over the rocky bones of the earth. That and several varieties of cactus. A hundred years of overgrazing had denuded the land, stripped it to the bone. Handfuls of Herefords still wandered over it, ripping up any green shoot from between the rocks. Herds of horses were turned loose on the open range to fare as best they could. Life on this land was hard, and the people could ill afford any suburban sentimentality about animals.

Still, the earth retained its own strength, but it was a strength not friendly to human enterprise. It was a land aloof and ascetic. It had suffered much under the hand of humans, and its austerity was beautiful but unyielding. Early in the morning when the sun was catching whatever nighttime moisture clung to the thick grey gourd leaves, there was a hint of the softness and abundance the land had once known. Wasps climbed drunkenly down into the yucca bloom caverns. Bees hummed around the chamisa and cactus blossoms. Jackrabbits stuck up their long ears along the irrigation canal. Among the cottonwoods, birds were calling. Walking out upon this world in its early morning joy, one caught the reflected light of fresh creation. The sun fell at a long gentle slope upon the waking world. But a few hours later it was beating straight down, pressing all life down into the hollows of shade.

It was only along the river or the canals that anything could grow. By the middle of the summer the river itself was low and sluggish as its waters were drained away to irrigate long, narrow alfalfa fields, cut narrower with each succeeding generation's inheritance.

Our neighbor, Mr. Suarez, an old bachelor, lived with his five fierce dogs that he fed a trough of biscuit dough every evening. He was considered the most successful farmer along the river valley. Besides his own fields, he leased all the land he could lay his hands on from the surrounding community and worked it with his new machinery from dawn to dark. He was neither Protestant nor Anglo, yet a sterner example of what is popularly called the Puritan work ethic never lived. Every moment of daylight was spent on his tractor, his mower, his baler. He raised acres of tomatoes and melons he could not possibly eat nor sell. He grew fruit trees that littered the ground with untouched pears and peaches. He dotted the fields with bale upon bale of alfalfa hay. In the winters he had pneumonia. And he did it all alone, a man in his late sixties. At first he was cautiously friendly to us, but after the incident with the ponies, he grew suspicious and edgy. It must have done his bitter old heart good to see the late-rising gringos hacking away at their little garden plot with pickaxes.

We had finally picked a spot right below the irrigation canal for a garden. There was plenty of seepage further down the slope, so we expected this spot to be fairly cooperative with our efforts. But we soon learned not to expect the ground to yield anything easily. It was rust red and tough as nails. The weeds that grew there had long since adapted their slender root systems to the nearly impenetrable soil. We confidently bought a new eight-horsepower rotary tiller and set to work to break the back of that patch. Instead the tiller broke. We discovered that the only way to break up the soil was literally with pickaxes.

During the winter months we shoveled truckload after truckload of manure out of a rancher's horse pen and dumped it on the garden. We hauled loads of sludge from the nearest town's sewer plant. By the following spring we could penetrate the soil with a shovel and use the tiller some.

Suarez was contemptuous of all our backbreaking efforts. His idea of farming this land was to wrestle it down, breaking it with a heavy plow. His furrows were yard-wide wounds, doused liberally with the strongest fertilizers he could buy. When the plants began to grow, he went over the field again with DDT. He irrigated extravagantly, being what was called the *majordomo* of the ditch commission, and kept a careful eye on our little trickle of water. In the fall there was no denying that he had the most abundant crops in the community. Truck after truck rolled away piled to the point of instability with his green alfalfa hay. He deposited box after box of dead-ripe tomatoes at our kitchen door that first summer to be put up on shares with him. He roasted mounds of green corn in his huge outdoor beehive oven. There was no denying his success—nor his complete lack of understanding of what we were trying to do.

Not that we had a particularly clear understanding ourselves. We simply had a vision of what we wanted the land to look like—rich, dark, crumbly soil inhabited by healthy earthworms and yielding up prize fruits and vegetables. Restored fertility. And given our scant resources, we didn't do badly. But to fulfill that vision on even a few acres would have taken a lifetime of hard work.

Like Hawthorne at Brook Farm, we soon began to complain that man was made for more than this. Of course, many among us took up the refrain before they had even tasted the "brutalizing" hard work. The few of us who were the first arrivals had set to work at once. We had brought with us several flats of carefully nurtured seedlings to be transplanted immediately since it was already the first week in June. But with the cat sleeping on them in the van, they had not survived the trip too well. Then Mr. Suarez donated some lusty tomato plants to us, beside which our own looked tubercular.

That first morning after we arrived, we awoke to a whistling wind sweeping up all the rain that had washed the hillsides so clean the evening before. Choking yellow dust filled the air, and it was cold enough to wear the heaviest clothes we had brought. Faye and I set about unpacking and cleaning indoors while Jack, Wayne, and Bob worked down in a field Suarez had recently plowed. We could see them from the house, leaning into the wind, trying to spread cottonseed meal on the iron-locked land. They came in chapped and raw themselves, overwhelmed with the futility of their work. We waited till evening when the wind died down to set out the plants.

Nothing much ever came of that garden. It sat on the dry slope, impervious to our unskilled attempts at irrigation. We refused to use commercial fertilizer, much to the bewilderment of Mr. Suarez. By July the area where the cottonseed meal had been spread was a lush green strip of bindweed with the most brilliant scarlet blossoms ever seen in that part of the country. Every species of insect in the county flocked there, but once again we refused insecticide, again to Suarez's consternation. It seemed to him that we were deliberately thwarting the agricultural process. His patch of corn, which we undertook to hoe in return for his having plowed up our field, flourished, while ours was withered and stunted. It was then that we set to work on the spot below the irrigation ditch with pickaxes.

But by then the agricultural experiment had been so disappointing that very few had any interest in investing in another piece of recalcitrant ground. Wayne, who had grown up on a farm, would hoe the cornfield, but working in a kitchen garden was not his idea of farming. Daniel would put in a few hours by way of an anthropological experiment, from which he concluded that earthworms were the wisest of all creatures since they could eat the dirt itself with no need for a middle man. Bob had worn out his enthusiasm that first windy day and was only interested in engineering a less primitive irrigation system. Don was waiting for his karma to come the right way round so he wouldn't unsettle the plants. Most of the others, except for Lillian, hardly knew the top from the bottom of a seedling and distinguishing a bean from a weed was beyond them.

Our theoretical hope had been to live outside the dollar economy that enslaved us to the mass-produced fruits of big business. We wanted to grow our own food, construct our own buildings, and in the end become a self-contained community that could ride out any apocalypse in style. With what we considered unusually far-sighted prudence, we made up lists of articles we knew we couldn't make in order to collect them against the day when Abernathy's General Store would no longer be operating. Needles and salt headed the list.

Nevertheless, no matter how indisposed any of us was to hard day-long labor, nor how unskilled and futile our attempts at farming and building, everyone was surprisingly generous with his or her money. We operated off of the savings accounts of two of our number who had held regular full-time jobs the year before. But whatever other supply of money trickled in—from families back home, part-time jobs in Santa Fe, hidden hoards—it was shared with astonishing nonchalance. This was as much an outcome of affluence as was the inability to stick to hard, grueling work. Money came, and went, easily. When large expenditures had to be made, everyone was quite content to leave those decisions in the hands of Jack, Lillian, and me, the chief contributors.

Although we frequently and out of necessity used the services of the local public health clinic, for some reason it never occurred to us to apply for food stamps, even though over half the population of the valley lived on them, until we were down to our last few dollars. That came during the dead of winter. Jack and I, as usual, were the ones subtly elected to do the applying. There had been much public controversy that year over how the government welfare agencies were to deal with communal applicants for the services. Therefore, rather than undergo the inspections and interrogations necessary for us all to apply as a household, we decided to apply only for ourselves and our children.

The four of us climbed into the frost-covered pickup one pale winter morning and started out for the county seat thirty-five miles south. We had heard that it was necessary to take along the children to prove their existence to the sometimes skeptical examiner. We were in a holiday mood. The idea of all that gratuitous play money that could be exchanged for real food filled us with excitement. The children made up imaginary grocery lists as we bounced along.

The building was an old house converted into small offices and a waiting room guarded by an officious Chicano woman with an elaborate hairdo. Several other people came and went as we sat waiting in the stripped-down room, thumbing through back issues of *Cosmopolitan* and reading the latest USDA publications of economy recipes. I grew more and more offended as case after case preceded us. At times like this my theoretical radicalism flared into pragmatic confrontation. It was obvious that the bustling receptionist, so busy pulling out drawers and snapping letterheads in and out of her typewriter, found us even more distasteful than most welfare cases. After all, we should know better. We were deliberately subverting the system. We were clearly capable of finding employment if we'd only go back to where we came from. And we felt just enough shame at receiving anything, especially something as essential as food, from the hands of a government we castigated, that we were edgy with defensiveness. Naturally we had gone over all the arguments in our favor—how we had contributed so many tax dollars so unwillingly over the years to the governmental coffers, most of which was spent against our expressed wishes for war machinery. We knew that the food stamp program was primarily a ploy to keep agribusiness booming with customers who otherwise would not be able to buy its products. Yet this exposure was painful and humiliating.

After an hour and a half the children grew restless, and I no longer demanded that they sit still and look at the magazines. Instead, I smiled maliciously as they raced around the small room and climbed on the furniture. We were the next ones to be called in for consultation.

The office we entered was a lean-to washroom that still held an old washing machine in the corner. The man behind the battered desk looked both unhappy and apprehensive. His black hair was slicked back in an outdated pompadour above a high narrow forehead. Dark heavy glasses hung sadly on his nose. His crisp white shirt ballooned around him, divided symmetrically by a dark tie. He was obviously unused to dealing with gringo food stamp applicants, but he was as polite and deferential as the receptionist had been haughty and rude. He explained the current rules to us thoroughly and filled out our application without comment. The children leaned silently against us and stared at him with big, uncomprehending eyes. It had always been their father and mother who were the ones dressed up in nice clothes asking questions of nervous students. Now things were turned around. It was hard to understand, both for the agent and for them.

Our application had to be processed, and it would be another two weeks before the U.S. Department of Agriculture decided to sprinkle its largesse upon the poor inhabitants of our county so that they could swamp Safeway with the little colored coupons.

Two weeks later was a somewhat warmer morning. We only had to drive the five miles to the local village this time, but when we arrived a line already extended outside the abandoned adobe building now used only for the monthly food stamp distribution. Again we felt awkward, though out of politeness the village people re-frained from staring at us, at least when we were look-ing their way. There was an expectant, almost festive air among them. Food stamp day meant relief, in more ways than one. The past few days had been spent eking out the last of the beans and masa. Tonight there would be canned spaghetti, canned peaches, sliced white bread.

The line inched forward, place being given to the oldest who had to sit on the benches that lined the wall. As we passed through the doorway, the same sad man we had seen in the county seat, dressed in an immac-ulate green suit and white shirt, wearily dispensed the pink booklets and checked off the recipients in his ledger. He did his job about as well as anyone in that situation could. I'm certain he heard many a hard-luck story in his daily rounds, both real and fabricated. Massive poverty is hard to hold up against. Shame and anger must be his daily lot. I hoped he found at least an occasional, if ambiguous, satisfaction.

A rail-thin old woman in a flowered voile dress covered by a sagging black cardigan shuffled to the counter in her felt house slippers and held out her bony brown fingers as he counted the coupons into them. "Diez, veinte, treinta. . . ."

Domingo, one of the town drunks, his face scrabbly with a two-day-old grizzled beard, blinked at the booklets and made an X beside his name in the ledger. Outside the building he was already looking for someone to sell them to for cash, the only currency the bar accepted.

The housewives watched like hawks as their allotment was counted out, then recounted them carefully before signing the book. They collected their children, hanging on their skirts, and hurried off to Abernathy's to pay off the bill they had run up last month and start on a fresh stock of canned goods.

We moved up to the counter. "Diez, veinte, treinta. . . ." He caught himself and began again. "Ten, twenty, thirty . . ." We signed the book briskly and made off in the pickup to the county-seat Safeway, where the lower prices more than made up for the gasoline expense. Oh the glories of cheese, canned sardines, pickles, and crackers. By noon we were munching away contentedly in the park, wrapped up to our eyes against the wind and watching the children at recess across the street.

It was not long before I adopted the attitude of the village housewives. While standing in the food stamp line was galling for Jack, it was as natural as going to the laundromat for me. I watched the booklets counted out as closely as the other women, though I never quite had the effrontery to recount them right under the sad man's nose. At the checkout stand in the supermarket things were a little touchier, and I did glance around to see who was behind me in line before I took out my pack of booklets. But the chances were fifty-fifty that they too were paying with food stamps. There is a certain female ferocity that goes with food-providing that precludes any possibility of humiliation.

On the way home we passed what had become a familiar sight—an old man tending his herd of goats while they grazed along the highway. His poncho hung down to his knees and he leaned on a long pole, watching us pass with a long, imperturbable stare. He had become as nearly as possible like the stony land itself, his dark, strong face having passed beyond every humiliation, beyond every pretense.

When we got back to the farm, we found Wilson there—a man who in many ways resembled the ancient goatherd. His body was lean, and his face sunburned and stony. His eyes, however, were quick, sharp, and contemptuous. Unlike the goatherd, he was far from imperturbable. Instead of becoming like the land, Wilson bought it. We all called him our benefactor as though it were an official title. He owned the farm we lived on. Born and raised on an even more barren farm somewhere south of us, he had for years nurtured a dream of coming back to this familiar landscape and putting his many talents to work. His mind was continually buzzing with building schemes, engineering projects, jewelry designs, paintings. Yet he had been trained for an academic profession that he felt paid him too well to abandon. He had suffered several tragedies in his life, including the loss of his wife, and he tried in an impatient way and with the stolid aid of his mother to bring up his three children.

He had decided to lend us his land without ever having laid eyes on us, negotiating with us through a mutual friend. In the weeks before we arrived we had built up a romantic picture of this generous, trusting benefactor. We had been living at the farm almost three months before we met him. Generous he had indeed been. But he would have lifted an ironic eyebrow at the "trusting" and called it foolhardy. In his impetuous way, Wilson was willing to enter into almost any exciting scheme, the more dramatic the better. But he could not abide failure.

When he heard that our garden had withered away, he sighed a long weary sigh. When some of the rabbits sickened and died, he breathed an almost audible prayer for patience. When repairs to the house came to a standstill for lack of funds, he stomped around the place pointing out improvements that could be made for no cash outlay. He would breeze in on a Saturday afternoon long enough to satisfy himself of our continued incompetence, and then drive off again in a cloud of ill-concealed disgust, leaving us feeling like ungrateful children.

We often challenged him to give up his tiresome administrative job and come live on the farm to provide the skill and leadership we so distinctly needed. To this he would smile benignly and shake his head. "Someone has to *pay* for the place, you know." Another cloud of guilt burst over our heads.

Wilson practiced bizarre economies. He never used butter or margarine, insisting loudly that bacon grease was quite sufficient as he poured it in great quantities over his pancakes. His children told us that he refused to have a refrigerator during the winter, leaving things out in the garage to freeze. He used cooking oil to slick down his sparse grey hair. He had an ancient Plymouth station wagon overhauled and then had it reupholstered with custom-made leather seat covers.

He was such a strange combination of so many opposites that at first we were simply fascinated by him. He had all the exaggerated personality distortions of a character out of Dickens. It didn't take long for the fascination to wear thin, however. Soon the others left Jack and me to deal with Wilson as best we could. Whenever he appeared in his whirlwind way, everyone drifted outside or into the dark corners, leaving him with his boots propped up near the wood stove and the two of us trying to strike an appropriate pose somewhere between jocular camaraderie and accountable foremen of a worthless crew of ne'er-do-wells.

Wilson liked to think of himself as one of us. "I know that everyone thinks I do nothing but live high on the hog," he would say with an injured tone, "but it's only to pay off this place. And I've my old mother to provide for. I'd give it up in a minute to be out here. Just think of me as one of the bunch though. I certainly don't expect any obsequiousness." And he would stare dolefully into the fire.

This particular evening as we rolled in, a light, feathery blanket of snow already covered the ground. We hoisted the boxes of food from the pickup, eyeing Wilson's little Corvair with apprehension. The yellow light fell out the kitchen door onto the snow; it would have warmed our weary hearts had we not known what waited us inside. As we lumbered in the door with the high-piled boxes, which ordinarily brought the whole crew dancing around us in anticipation, only Sally looked up at us blackly from the stove where she was stirring a stew. Wilson was bustling around the kitchen, opening cans of what he thought would be a welcome addition to the pot.

He stopped momentarily to investigate our new food hoard.

"Peanut butter?" he queried, holding up a three-pound jar. "I should have thought you could make that in the blender using real peanuts. And white sugar! I thought you people were health food nuts. Here, Sally, I think it's time for these to go in now." And he handed her a jar of pickled artichoke hearts he had brought along as his personal contribution to the meal.

During supper we began again trying to convince Wilson to allow us to use the irrigated fields in the spring. Suarez had been leasing them ever since Wilson had bought the place.

"Really, Wilson, I don't see how you can expect us to do anything without water." Jack's voice was getting a rough edge to it. "We only manage to get a trickle for the garden because Suarez is the *majordomo* and winks at it since he's afraid he'll lose the lease on the alfalfa otherwise."

"Yes, that Suarez is crafty, isn't he." And Wilson chuckled with appreciation for our thriving neighbor. Obviously, he was more impressed with Suarez's solitary success than with our poor scrabbling efforts.

"If you really believed in what we were doing . . ." Jerry for once spoke up, determined to push the point home.

"You misunderstand me, you misunderstand me." Wilson held up a defending hand. "What would you work it with? You've no equipment, and heaven knows I've no money to be buying any."

Everyone held his breath, hoping that Jerry wouldn't say "horses" and bring up the recent unpleasantness with Suarez over the ponies. But he only muttered something incomprehensible under his breath and attacked an artichoke savagely.

Wilson went on. "Now I know you're all thinking I'm against you and don't trust your abilities." He paused long enough for the point to sink home that he would be perfectly justified in such opinions. "But after supper we'll walk down the road to the river and I'll point out to you a strip of mine that has been approved for irrigation, in fact already has a ditch to it and a gate."

However, the group that assembled outside the kitchen door after supper included only Wilson, Jack, Jerry, and me. The others had had a full measure of Wilson's magnanimity and were creeping in by the fire as we set off down the lane, now obscured with snow, towards the river. The flakes fell thickly on our caps and hunched shoulders, and our boots kicked up feathery clouds of white dust. It was a beautiful night. The world seemed suspended in a steely blue light, the light of a snow-diffused twilight. The whole sky seemed to be in a continual state of falling. A white world closed in.

Of course, when we got to the strip Wilson had been telling us about, we could do no more than mentally mark its position in order to come back and examine it later. The snow covered the land, but we could tell by the fence posts that it was a rather small strip, no more than two or three acres.

All of a sudden the dogs put up a tremendous yelping and barking. They were lunging and backing off from a dark shape we could only just make out near the fence line further down the road. We waded through the gloom to investigate it. There, barely discernible through the dark and drifting snow, was the stiffening hide of a donkey, one we recognized as having spent the summer grazing in Suarez's alfalfa.

"What's this!" I cried, meaning not what but why.

Wilson smiled crookedly and put out a gloved hand to touch the grey hide. It swung against the fence and the piled-up snow cascaded softly down.

"Suarez," he said, "kills a donkey every winter so his dogs'll have some meat." He nodded his head in respect to the farsighted Suarez.

I turned my back and started the walk home. My toes were freezing in my boots and I felt frozen inside. All night long that stiffening donkey hide flapped against the fence inside my head.

Dante, exiled from his native Florence and forced during the last and most productive years of his life to depend on the charities of a patron, wrote of "how salty the bread tastes in others' houses, and how hard is the going up and down of others' stairs." We too chafed under the restraint of not living on our own place, of having our decisions frustrated. Failure was a blacker fear when it meant failing your patron. How we longed for one clear moment of unalloyed gratitude, to be able to say the word "benefactor" without the load of irony it carried for us now. Though we came to know every slope, every arroyo, every defiant plant that grew on that land, our love for it was forever unconsummated. It belonged to someone else.

Not that the land cared about such questions. But there were people in northern New Mexico who would have disputed Wilson's right to the property—proponents of the original land-grant theory who declared that the land ceded to them by the Spanish crown centuries before had been illegally taken from the Spanish settlers in shady deals by Anglos. And back behind those claims were the rights of the Indians who had been cruelly driven from the land by the Spanish settlers. They had not even the Western concept of land ownership to use as their appeal. The earth was their mother in a way that had degenerated into sentimentality for us. Yet the land had yielded to them as scantily as it did to us. Our shriveled little garden had more in common with the dry land farms of the Southwest Indians than with Suarez's forced bounty. At Mesa Verde are tiny ears of corn, preserved for centuries—the undeniable record of the returns given for patient tending.

Of course there was no question of going back to that sort of life on the land. Our senses have deteriorated far below the sharpness necessary to hunt and to gather wild food. Besides, the buffalo, the berries, the fish had all gone with the Indians. And no matter how romantic the vision, we would not recove r it.

Our dilemma was hopeless. Small wonder the Robin Hood stories held the same appeal for us they had for the late Middle Ages, when ideas about land ownership were also in flux. How lovely to return to the forest, living off its natural abundance and filling in the chinks with booty from the bad guys—a life with a great deal more flair than food stamps offered.

For us, though, there were no Sherwood Forests, only the daily butting of our heads against the crumbling adobe wall of our benefactor.

6

You are dust and to dust you shall return.

—Genesis 3:19

We are dying, we are dying, we are all of us dying
and nothing will stay the death-flood rising within us
and soon it will rise on the world, on the outside world.

We are dying, we are dying, piecemeal our bodies are dying
and our strength leaves us,
and our soul cowers naked in the dark rain over the flood,
cowering in the last branches of the tree of our life.

—D. H. Lawrence, "The Ship of Death"

The sidewalk leading up the hill to the clinic was broken and heaved by the frozen ground. I had to pick my way carefully among the thawed spots in the snow. I must take care not to fall.

The clinic was north of the courthouse and one of the newer buildings in this town generally left behind in the backwash of progress. I knew by report that the woman at the reception desk was a dragon. If I could make it past her, there would be friendly, helpful faces down the left corridor, where the women lined up once a week for birth control pills and pregnancy examinations.

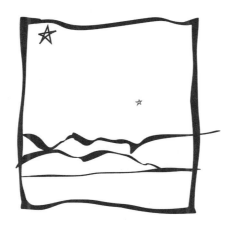

As she pushed the forms across the counter to me, I could easily read the question in her eyes: why wasn't I where I belonged, on the other side of town in some cozy private waiting room? I swallowed at my nausea and tried meekly to focus on the forms before me. I was in no such feisty mood as I had been at the food stamp office.

"Occupation: Beekeeper."

My mind plummeted back to an old-fashioned romantic novel I had read in adolescence, *The Keeper of the Bees*. Lots of warm hillsides and fragrant meadows. Not much about the interminable scraping of bee gum from frames, the angry hum of bees caught in the hair. Oh, for a sun-warmed hillside. Outside the plate glass of the reception room bare branches swung in the early spring wind and the dirty slush hardened into packed ice. Would it ever be warm again?

The receptionist eyed the form critically, then glanced at me with a look that gave me to understand she didn't believe a word of it, and motioned vaguely toward the left corridor. I'd made it past the first barrier.

I took my place in the row of chairs that lined the hallway, thankful for a place to sit and breathe deeply. The walls were postered with pictures designed to educate the poor and ignorant about medical care for their babies—inoculations, vaccinations, emergency treatment for accidental poisoning. And information about various birth control methods. Fat healthy babies smiled down at me alongside diagrams of IUDs. I tried not to look at either one and concentrated on the women around me.

Some stared stolidly out over their swollen abdomens, sighing shallowly from time to time. Others remonstrated ineffectually with toddlers who played hide-and-seek under the chairs and accepted smugly the compliments from their neighbors on the bright eyes, the curly hair, the cleverness of their offspring. Still others sat smoking and swinging a nervous leg, eyeing the little bodies tumbling around them with marked suspicion.

The nurses hurried back and forth from room to room, counting out pills, sticking needles in round little bottoms, explaining with extreme care the necessity of taking every pill on time. Brisk, clean, efficient. Why had I ever left that world, I groaned inwardly. I knew almost all the nurses. Each of them was widowed, their children gone from home. Devoted to their work, they found their duty plainly before them, simple and clean with few ambiguities. And so pressed for time they hadn't the luxury of introspection. The one who visited our village every month smiled as she whisked by me.

"It won't be long," she said encouragingly. And it wasn't. No longer than the waits in the cozy private waiting rooms across town.

In the dressing cubicle I slipped shivering into a sadistic little plastic shirt. All around me in the other cubicles the women were talking back and forth and giggling at their predicament. I began to tremble violently.

It wasn't long till my name was called and another nurse ushered me into the examining room. The doctor, her face plain and comforting as a potato, indicated the table, and I scooted myself onto it.

"Now then, what seems to be your problem?"

"I, uh, haven't had a regular period in three months. Just some irregular bleeding."

"Let's take a look."

She pushed and prodded and poked at my tense body, all the time her eyes staring noncommittally across the table.

"I was afraid I might be pregnant," I began.

"No need to be afraid," she said. "You definitely are."

"But I *can't* be," I protested. "I've had an IUD for a year now."

"It must have transmigrated," she replied. "That happens fairly often. They're not foolproof."

"But what does that mean? That is, where is it and what—"

"It probably moved up through the vagina and is stuck somewhere in the uterus along with the fetus. How much have you been bleeding?"

"Intermittently. Not a lot. But will this damage the baby? I mean, is there a chance something will be wrong with it?"

She drew in her bottom lip and looked thoughtful. "The chances are good it will be perfectly normal. I can't guarantee it, of course. However, if you're concerned about that possibility, I can get you into Bernalillo County hospital. Only an overnight trip and it can all be taken care of."

"We hadn't intended," I choked out, "to have any more children. I thought the IUD . . ."

"I understand." She patted my knee. "It's up to you to decide. Really I think it will be all right. However, if the possibility upsets you, I can handle all the arrangements at the hospital. No trouble. But you must decide soon. The cut-off time is sixteen weeks and I think you're getting near that already."

"I'll let you know," I said weakly. "I'll have to talk it over with my husband."

"Sure," she answered. "The nurse will give you the usual vitamins and nausea tablets if you need them." And she hurried off to the next patient.

I picked my way even more carefully back down the broken sidewalk, clutching the boxes of pills inside my coat pocket, trying not to think till I had made it safely back home. As I went up the hill I had only been full of vague suspicions and annoyance. Now it was sure. Something live inside me, something to protect. All my other feelings would have to be sorted out later. Anger, fear, worry, disappointment, excitement, anticipation, hope. Now I only concentrated on getting down the hillside without slipping and falling.

Back at home, everyone thought the news immensely entertaining, though all of them would have gone to almost any lengths to avoid being saddled with pregnancy and a child. The same old jokes and comments their parents and grandparents had made in similar situations were pulled out gleefully for my benefit. Why people should react with such glowing and clumsy goodwill was beyond me. The possibility of impending abortion, however, was no laughing matter. But that was my problem and Jack's.

The matter was never much in doubt from the beginning.

"She says she thinks it'll be all right?" he asked anxiously.

"Yes. Of course there's no way of knowing really."

"It might be a boy," he said guardedly.

"Yes. Perhaps."

"I really can't have the final say, you know." He wrapped his coat around me as we walked down the road to the river. "Whichever way you want to go. If you don't want to take the chance, I'm certainly with you. Or if you do."

I was several days deciding. If only she had said the chances were fifty-fifty it would have been clear. But the possibilities seemed greater for a whole, well child.

I fought against it with every ounce of educated rationality I had. But there is something so tempting about secret, hidden, growing things. How would it turn out? What if it were a son? And the girls were excited too. I had cautioned them against assuming that every-thing was all right, explaining carefully all the potential hazards. Yet their eyes gleamed as they looked at me expectantly.

"We'll help, Mother. We'll take care of it."

Probably I had already decided the morning I had walked so carefully down the hill from the clinic. I told the doctor the next week to forget about the arrangements at the hospital. She nodded and made a regular appointment for me the next month at the clinic.

Once more life was full of anticipation and hope. I no longer cared who came or went on the farm. I had my own secret concern. My body became of intense interest to me, every new sign of advancing pregnancy filling me with satisfied accomplishment. It was all right. Another day and it had grown a little more. The life inside me was like a sign of new hope, a new beginning. A child of promise.

The weather began to turn warm at last. Daily the sun moved higher in the sky from its winter hibernation in the southern sector. More minutes of light crept in at the end of each day. We began breaking the ground for the new garden.

The plans for the irrigated strip closer to the river had never worked out. By spring Jerry had left, his heart broken, and we had neither horses nor machinery to work it nor enough strong bodies to make up for the lack. But we were expanding the garden from the year before. All our efforts in our neighbors' corrals and at the city sludge dump were not going to be fruitless.

The winter had been full of sickness. Sally had had to go to Denver for an operation. She came back on the bus still shaky and weak. "I'd better get a job in town," she told us. "I'd be no good out here at all. I'm not strong enough to work outdoors, and I'd only be a drain on everyone else." We all agreed it was best for her to be somewhere reasonably warm and clean. But we all missed her whimsy that kept us cheered. We would much rather have given up Simon and his unremitting gloom.

Then sickness struck us all. From the first summer we had all been troubled intermittently with severe diarrhea and nausea. Thinking that our problem came in by way of the flies that swarmed around the dilapidated outhouse, we spent several weeks during the first summer designing and building a new one—a lovely little A-frame with screens on the windows and a wooden floor. Blasting a hole out of the rock with dynamite had been the high point of Bob's New Mexico adventure. Nevertheless, although the sanitary facilities were much improved, the problem persisted. Periodically we all got sick with fits of violent vomiting, diarrhea, chills, and sometimes fever. In fact, it grew even worse during the winter when all the flies had long since died off.

It was efficient Lillian who, after suffering a long bout herself, took water samples from our tap to be tested by the health department. The report came back: paratyphoid. We investigated the source of our water supply. The well reservoir was full of all sorts of dead creeping things, including a mouse. But that wasn't the real source of the problem. The well itself was filled from the seepage of the irrigation canal and Suarez's horse pond, no more than twenty feet on the other side of our fence. The well was polluted.

After this discovery, we hauled drinking water from town or boiled the well water. But the effects of paratyphoid take a long time to get over.

By the end of the winter only our own family and Wilson's teenage son—whom he'd left with us when the grandmother could no longer handle him—remained on a day-in, day-out basis. Others came and went. We had frequent visitors, sometimes strangers passing through, looking for a place to embark on a similar project themselves. But broken relationships between men and women and broken health had ravaged our original community.

Still I was hopeful. Our little family had grown tighter through it all. Let everyone else go! We knew we could depend on one another. It had been a year of hell—the poverty, the sickness, the cold, the hard work, the desertions—but we had come through. And now there would be a new one amongst us.

Jane, our seven-year-old, who had chosen not to go to school, was with me constantly. She watched the goats after I had staked them every morning below the garden. We spent sunny afternoons scraping the accumulations of bee gum from secondhand frames.

"There are ten frames in a super. We've done seven already. How many more do we have to do?" I would ask. "We've put six tomato plants in each row and we've made three rows. How many is that?"

"Enough," would be her obstinate reply.

Gradually the garden took shape. Out of our new hotbed I transferred small lettuces, cabbage, broccoli, and cauliflower in all shades of green. We mulched with straw against what we knew would be the dry early summer. Once again plans began to germinate in our heads. A new house. We could at least start on the foundation; there were free rocks and clay in abundance. We made up lists of honey customers and scrubbed out gallon jars in anticipation of the golden flow.

Several weeks later when I was standing at the sink over the lunch dishes, I noticed the dark red trickle down my leg. I carefully wiped it away before Jane could see, told her to finish washing up, and went quickly to the bedroom. I lay down on the bed and stared at the ceiling, my head spinning and buzzing. I didn't even formulate any words in my mind, didn't tell myself to be calm or not to worry. I simply lay there and waited, like any animal in danger waits alert for the next thing that is going to happen. But nothing more happened. I lay there for an hour, then turned cautiously onto my side and began to breathe deeply again and to plan. The next clinic wasn't for four days. What did this mean? What should I do?

Jack had been working for one of the local ranchers. When he came in late in the afternoon I sent him off to the nearest gas station to call the nurse in town.

"Have her stay in bed," she instructed. "And unless the bleeding gets any worse, we'll see her in clinic next Tuesday."

I stayed in bed and the problem seemed to disappear. It had only been a bad scare. At the clinic the doctor examined me, frowning in concentration.

"It's still growing," she reported. "There's nothing really to be done. Just stay off your feet as much as possible. And if the bleeding gets bad, come into town immediately and the nurse-midwife will handle everything. She'll examine you and make the decision."

Shaken, we left the clinic and climbed in the old pickup. Jack carefully avoided every chuckhole on the way home.

Each day now there was only one question in my mind. Would we make it? I woke up every morning, checked myself for bleeding, tottered into the kitchen and sat down again. Then I fixed breakfast slowly, allowing myself no more than five minutes at a time on my feet. After the other children were off to school, Jane and I would go back to bed for another hour. If things were going well after that, we would scrape some more honey frames.

Watching Jack, almost dropping from weariness now that he had all his work and most of mine to do too, I was torn apart with indecision. Perhaps we should have gone ahead with the abortion. We couldn't afford this invalidism. Maybe I should simply get up, continue with my part of the work, and take the consequences. Besides, my determined mind gave itself a shake, I'm a strong, healthy woman who has borne two other children with no problems. I'm simply overdramatizing the situation.

So one morning early in April I crept cautiously down to the garden. I worked all morning, setting tomatoes into the cold frame. Nothing happened. My heart lifted again. It was going to be all right.

The next two days I worked warily in the garden, irrigating, planting, hoping. On the third day, late in the afternoon, I stood up from patting down the final row of peas and blood gushed from me like a torrent, saturating my jeans and boots.

"Quick, Jane, quick. Go get Daddy." I was crying and trembling and she seemed uncertain whether to stay or go until I screamed at her again to hurry.

I went doubled over up to the house, holding the bulge of my abdomen as though to protect it from whatever was happening inside. I stripped off my soaked clothes and lay down, shivering and sobbing under the blankets. A few minutes later Jack was there. Alice had just come in from school and he set her to heating some water to wash me. By the time I was cleaned up, the bleeding had almost stopped. I dressed, Jack left instructions for the children in case we didn't get back that night, and we started the hour-long drive into town.

It was dark when we got there. He rang up the nurse-midwife from a service station and she arranged to meet us at the clinic. There was no dragon to face this time, no waiting women lining the hall, just the dark clinic and one lighted examining room. The nurse shook her head.

"It seems to have pretty well stopped now. And there's still a heartbeat. Why don't you stay in town tonight, just in case, and I'll look at you again tomorrow."

Out in the dark street again, we held onto one another tightly and considered. At least there was a temporary respite and some reason to hope. We decided to treat ourselves to a warm, comfortable motel room with a real bath provided amply with hot running water.

Lying between the crisp clean sheets, knowing that if I swung my feet over the side of the bed a curly carpet instead of gritty concrete would touch my toes, that I could walk into the bathroom a few feet away and wash myself in gallons of hot water, I began to feel that nothing could touch me here. Those horrible explosions of blood belonged to that stark, uncontrollable world where things crept up on us—dirt, sweat, smoke, splinters, disease. Here, in the midst of all this comfort that for most of my life had been my natural habitat, I had the upper hand. It was safe.

I snuggled down under the blankets and slept, hour after hour, waking only when Jack brought in a sack of apples, cheese, and crackers. He had made a fast trip home early in the morning to see that the children were all right. Mrs. Chavez, a close neighbor, was keeping an eye on them.

In the afternoon I went by the clinic again. The bleeding had almost stopped altogether.

"Go on home," the nurse advised us. "But stay in bed as much as possible." She didn't say it very hopefully. She was used to dealing with women for whom staying in bed all day was about as possible as flying to the moon.

I hated to leave the motel room, but I couldn't stay there for the next four months. And we had already spent more money than we could afford on this expedition. We bounced home, watching a perfect sunset. As we rolled into the yard, the kitchen door filled with three expectant faces. Are you all right? Have you come home to us? Their relief was gleeful as they saw both of us climb down out of the truck.

The kitchen was a wreck from their efforts to get supper ready. We sat down to a boisterous meal. Jane settled herself against my side. It had been only twenty-four hours since I left. Here I was back again. Nothing had changed. The problems were still there.

This was not the last of the terrified dashes to the hospital, Jack shooting anguished glances at me as he geared down, eased over wash-outs in the road, and tried to make up the time on open stretches. Emergency room. Examination. Still alive, still a heartbeat. Go home. Complete bed rest. This will have to work itself out.

For six weeks I was in bed almost constantly. Jane was my nurse. Quick, attentive, long-suffering. She read what books she could to me after I had grown tired of reading myself. I worked on house plans, drawing and measuring and re-drawing. When all this was over. . . .

Between emergency trips all was calm. The nurse had begun teaching us the Lamaze breathing techniques, which we practiced assiduously. We all spent time searching for suitable names. This special child must have a special name. The girls described in inaccurate detail the care they would take of their baby brother. I smiled but did not encourage their fantasy.

I watched my body like a cat at a mousehole, ready to pounce on the least sign of hope or despair. I closed my eyes and tried to concentrate on what was going on inside the dark cavern of my body. Surely I should know, should be able to pick up some echo from within.

But I was worried. The baby didn't seem like it was growing as it should. At least I wasn't as big as I had been in previous pregnancies. Perhaps it was simply the lack of normal activity.

The spring came on, warm one day, windy the next. The bees were out, reaping every early flower. The peas Jack planted were up. Every day was one day closer.

On one of the windy days I was watching the sand whip through the air and the branches of the new-leafed trees bend straight out over the irrigation ditch when I heard a rasping, scrabbling noise across the room. Not a rat, I prayed, catching my breath. It was high up somewhere, almost on the ceiling. I picked up a shoe beside the mattress and waited, ready to heave it at whatever varmint had invaded my room. The noise stopped, then began again. Finally I saw it. A giant centipede, at least a foot long, was descending the opposite wall in uncertain fits and starts. Its weight was against it as it skidded from toehold to toehold in the rough concrete wall. I lifted the shoe and aimed it as well as I could from my bed. It hit one end of the creature, knocking it down the remaining length of wall where it fell in a bent heap; then it started skittering first one way and then another aimlessly. I screamed for Jane who was in the kitchen. I was in terror that the thing would find its way to the bed. At last Jane came in trailing her dish towel.

"Watch out," I cried, pointing to the centipede. "Get something quick. A big stick."

She ran outside to the woodpile, picked up a hefty chunk, and came running in again. The prospect of getting close enough to hit the creature frightened her, however, and she simply hurled the stick at it with all her might and ran out to get more. By the time the broken body of the centipede had stopped its frenzied scurrying, the floor was littered with firewood. When it was over we huddled together on the bed and cried—at the twisted, twitching, hideous form, at the fear, at its long dying. We left it there till Jack came in, incredulous at its size, and removed it at the end of one of the sticks.

I spent more time outside after that, lying on the new grass under the trees. Waiting, waiting. There was nothing else to do. Some days I was hopeful; other times my mind was as dulled as any animal.

It was the middle of May on a Sunday. I had had some minor bleeding in the morning, only to discover that the small, ivory-colored coil of the IUD had expelled itself. The bleeding stopped. At last, I breathed deeper, it's over. It's truly going to be all right.

I walked down to the garden and propped myself beneath a tree, planning what I would do now, how I could help. An hour later I began to notice small but unmistakable contractions. About twenty minutes apart, I judged. I didn't even dare shift positions. I waited. They continued. Grew closer. It was midafternoon before I climbed slowly back to the house, checked the overnight bag I always kept ready, and sent Jack to call the nurse.

This was the last time, I knew. Wordless all the way to town, we held fast to each other's hand. We drew up in front of the hospital this time. The lawn was already filled with roses. The sun was heavy and yellow.

Inside the nurse was waiting. Sunday afternoon was slow and leisurely at the hospital. I was put in a labor room this time, doing the breathing exercises and holding tight to Jack.

"I'm not going to give you anything, not even an aspirin," the nurse-midwife told us. "There's still a chance the baby can make it. Only a slight one. It's so early. Still, we want to give it every chance."

I nodded, working hard at breathing right, catching the pain cleanly on its edge. Jack stood beside me, his eyes big and dark.

"Now!" he would say, feeling my muscles tighten under his hand.

Two hours. The characteristic pause in contractions that occurs just before the big push. Jack rushed for the nurse. I was being wheeled down the hall, Jack still rehearsing the instructions with me. The nurse and I disappeared inside the swinging doors. There was a bright light. I was shaking and cold. The nurse looked at me from between my knees, which seemed like mountains looming up in white draperies.

"Push," she commanded. I pushed.

"Again, harder," she said sharply. I bore down hard. I felt as if I was going to turn inside out.

"Push," she shouted. And this time with all my strength I pushed out into the world the secret I had borne for over half a year. I felt it slide inside me, give way, then rush forth, and with a cry I hardly recognized as my own, tearing along my lungs, expelling the weeks of anguish and fear. It was only an inarticulate scream; it meant it's over.

She told me immediately. "It's dead," she said. "It was dead before it was born. A little boy. Very small."

She laid it aside and was busy delivering the afterbirth. I didn't try to see it. "Push," she repeated periodically. And I pushed between great heaving sobs. She said nothing more, but patted my ankle from time to time. When it was over she sent me away with another nurse.

My grief seemed to fill me up more than the child ever had. It was heavy and its bitterness unambiguous. To have come so close, to have lost what we worked for so hard. A boy. A son. I truly did not know how I could bear the loss.

Early the next morning I had surgery. It was shortly after dawn when the doctor slipped into my room.

"Are you certain you want to go through with this?" she asked. "A tubal ligation is a very final thing."

"Yes. I couldn't live through another disappointment like this. I have my two children. That's the quota."

Friends came to see me, some of the old communitarians. I couldn't speak without weeping. They went away again. They think it's strange, I told myself. One less baby in the world at this point in history is only a blessing. I should have given it up earlier. I ground my teeth and choked.

Two days later I went home. I wept unremittingly. My parents came. I told my mother I could not bear it. She said I would learn how.

7

So he drove out the man; and he placed at the east of the garden of Eden cherubims, and a flaming sword which turned every way, to keep the way of the tree of life.

—Genesis 3:24

Yet, after all, let us acknowledge it wiser, if not more sagacious, to follow out one's day-dream to its natural consummation, although, if the vision has been worth having, it is certain never to be consummated otherwise than by a failure.

—Hawthorne, *The Blithedale Romance*

Summer began again, full of feverish activity. The garden, three times the size of the first summer's, promised at least a fair crop. We extracted honey weekly now, taking turns at the crank handle and watching the golden liquid flow like a miracle from the spout into the gallon jars. And we worked on the house, hauling rock, trampling adobe in a mud pit, drying bricks in the front yard.

We had all three of Wilson's children with us now, and occasional passers-through. But I shrank morbidly from outside human contact. People were an almost in supportable burden. I saw vehicles draw up to the front gate with disgust and revulsion.

"People are so predictable," I protested to Jack when he mentioned bringing someone new onto the farm. "It's never anything different, never anything new. Always the same petty stupidities."

My attitude angered Jack. It was ironical, I thought. Here was Jack, naturally gregarious, yet with a volatile, explosive temper that sometimes frightened people away, linked with me, who would outwardly put up with multitudes of failings while secretly despising people in my heart.

Wilson, who had scarcely shown his face during the spring, now came down almost every weekend, bringing friends with him. He had been put off by my pregnancy, making no attempt to hide his opinion that our decision against an abortion was stupid and senseless at a time like this. He never mentioned the miscarriage at all. The friends he brought were well-to-do, more often women than not, excited at the prospect of seeing a real hippie farm in operation.

Strangely enough, I resented these people far less than the ragged regiments of dreamers that rolled into the yard to stay a day or two and scout around for a prospective paradise. I was contemptuous of their amorphous plans, the hope that glowed on their faces for a blurry, brighter tomorrow, the sentimental, bastardized Eastern mysticism they espoused.

"You'll never make it," I muttered under my breath. "You're not tough enough."

I kept a daily, detailed diary, but it very purposefully contained only incidents of the nonhuman world. I saved accounts of the garden, the weather, the animals, the sun and moon, but I obstinately refused to let any human vicissitude enter the story. What people did or did not do was now beside the point.

In short, I was well on my way to becoming a first-rate Stoic. My credentials lay in my ability to take almost anything—30°-below winters around a wood stove, disease, hard work, welfare examiners, dirt, disappointment, death. Nothing could touch me. I cultivated calmness in the face of calamity. My life belonged to me; I was responsible for it.

We worked hard through the summer, but still there seemed to be a blight on our efforts. Wilson, who at first had been excited about our new building plans, was now dissatisfied.

"There's not the right amount of straw in these bricks," he protested. "They won't dry right that way." "You ought to haul rocks from further down by the river." I could see the handwriting on the as yet unfinished wall.

Nothing we did pleased him. He grew more irritable with each succeeding visit. We began to see that there was only one way to solve our hassles with Wilson: we must try to buy a few acres of the property where we could build a house in peace and release ourselves from this tenant-farmer burden. He was obviously shocked when we presented our plan to him, but promised to think about it.

One day a lone straggler appeared in the yard, his hair long and matted and his shirt thrown over his shoulder along with a day pack containing his few belongings. He had come from a commune we knew of further north in the mountains. A band of drunk local studs had invaded the place, killed one of the commune members, carried off one of the women in their car trunk and then raped her and left her not far from town. Everyone was leaving, he said, fleeing. We fed him and he went on, not knowing where, following the road.

Meanwhile, a school friend of ours from the Midwest, Margaret, came to stay for a few weeks. She had with her a hitchhiker she'd picked up while camping in a national park.

"This is Keith," she introduced him. "He's from Florida. He teaches English in a junior college there. And he's published some poetry."

Keith was big and muscular, eager to make himself useful. We mentally assessed the number and size of rocks he could haul in a day.

After supper he told his own story. "I'm just sort of knocking around now. I lost my family. My wife and two little girls were killed in a car wreck last spring. I'm just trying to get it together again."

We were shocked that anyone could sustain such a blow with such equanimity.

"Sure, you can stay," Jack told him. "I know you don't want to be making any permanent decisions now. But unload your gear, we'll put you to work, and you can see how you feel about it after a while."

Keith was rather rough, especially with Wilson's boy, and I found it difficult to think of him in any poetical setting. But this wasn't the nineteenth century, I reminded myself. And he worked hard, sticking with the job all morning long, then ready to go again after lunch.

One day he asked to borrow the van; he had some errands to run in town. Keith returned late in the afternoon. He'd bought some work clothes at a secondhand store.

I was relieved to have an extra pair of hands around the place. Visions of the new house standing snug and warm by the first snow flickered through my mind as I watched Jack and Keith unloading the rocks at the new site. I wasn't happy with Jack's response to Keith, however. They were together constantly, talking, talking, talking. I only hovered around the periphery of their attention, squawlike. I'm not enough for Jack, I thought. He needs something more. Other people. It made me angry to think that he found Keith's company so congenial that they sat up every evening till after midnight while I went to bed alone.

About a week later, when Jack and I were down in the garden hoeing, a big white car pulled onto the bridge.

"Who's that?" I asked warily, shading my eyes against the sun.

We were sometimes harassed by cars full of drunken villagers out on hippie-heckling excursions. Jack turned to look. A man in a dark uniform emerged from the car. He waved and came toward us. Jack propped his hoe against the fence and went to meet him. I continued hoeing. I had no truck with policemen around here. I watched them move on up toward the house. What could it be? I counted off all the possibilities in my mind. Search? Someone we knew in an accident? What? I kept hoeing till I saw the car drive off, then rushed up to the house. There was no need to ask. Everyone was around me trying to speak at once.

"You'll never believe it," they gasped. "It's Keith. They took him away. His wife—she came for him."

"But . . . she's dead," I protested.

"Didn't look like it to me, the way she grabbed him."

When Keith had seen the police drive up, he had ducked into the big bedroom, Alice told us. He had changed into the clothes he was wearing when he first arrived.

Meanwhile the policeman had shown Jack a picture of Keith to identify.

"He's not under arrest or anything," the policeman assured Jack. "It's just that his wife's looking for him." Jack had been startled at the woman in a tight pantsuit and piled-up hairdo who was just getting out of the car. She looked old enough to be Keith's mother. "Says he disappeared about two weeks ago."

At that moment Keith opened the kitchen door and came slowly down the steps, his eyes on the ground. By the time he reached the gate, the woman had thrown herself upon him. "Oh, Keith honey, where have you been?" He put his arms rather reluctantly around her and they moved off to the car.

Jack was finally shaken out of his amazement enough to run after him. "Hey, man. What shall we do with your things? Don't you want to take them with you?"

Keith shook his head, still unwilling to raise his eyes to Jack's. "You keep 'em," he said in an undertone. "Maybe I'll be back."

With that they all climbed into the big white car and headed off toward town.

That was the last we ever saw or heard of Keith. In his backpack, which he had left in the bedroom along with his other things, we found a classic letter, written to his wife but never mailed, explaining how he had taken their money out of savings, how she would undoubtedly hate him, how he felt compelled to do this. We inherited the fruits of the savings account: an expensive backpack, a down sleeping bag, and an alpine tent. The letter had not been addressed, so there was no way of returning them.

"I don't think he wanted her to know he had them," Margaret said. We were still sitting around the supper table, stunned by the scene. "Gee, you guys, I'm sorry. When I brought him here I didn't know . . ."

"No way you could have," I said. "How strange. Of course he never was a teacher. Or a poet." I felt relieved about that.

"Or a father."

It was a little scary that we had been so easily conned. Even I, with my deep-rooted suspicions of human nature, so well watered by the past year's experience, had not been able to spot the deception, even when all of us had openly wondered at certain incongruities in his actions. Here I thought I had built up a wall of skepticism around myself that made me invulnerable to almost anything. And I had been taken in by a stupid, obviously fabricated story. I wasn't careful enough yet.

Jack's concern was elsewhere. "I wonder what'll happen to him now."

"He'll never get another chance, that's for sure," Margaret said.

———

The incident with Keith shook us badly. On its heels came another shock. Our oldest daughter, Alice, had to have an operation.

"Just a simple hernia repair," the doctor assured us. "I know your circumstances are somewhat," he paused and arranged the pen beside the telephone, "straitened. I'll only charge half my normal fee."

It was generous and I thanked him. But even half the fee was money we didn't have. Family-planning and maternity clinics were one thing. A ten-year-old with a funny lump on her otherwise flat little belly was something else. We couldn't forever depend on the public services of a county already overloaded with poverty.

I was frantic as I drove home. It was *my* life. Why wasn't I able to control it better? There must be a way. My mind darted down one path after another. At the end of each was either a wall, a dark question, or the lurking monster that wheezed, "Give up. Leave. It's over."

That possibility made me tremble so I could hardly drive. "No!" I almost shouted aloud. "I will not. I can not."

Every evening now was spent going over the tortuous paths that opened out from our present standing place. Borrow the money for the operation from our parents? An obvious defeat. Borrow the money from Wilson? We choked on that one. He hadn't even mentioned again our offer to buy a piece of land from him. To borrow would be like shopping at the company store. Finally: get a job. That meant leaving. At least one of us. The farm was too far out from anywhere to commute. And what kind of job? The unemployment rate in the county was eighteen percent and upward. We had managed to get by during the summer on our honey sales and food stamps. Now what?

Jack ran his hands through his thick dark hair and sighed. "I guess we better go into town tomorrow. See what we can find there."

He got out a suit that had been packed away in plastic for over a year. I ironed a dress and unearthed some stockings.

The girls danced around us and clapped their hands. "Gee, Mama, you all look just like you *used* to." Jack and I grinned grimly at one another.

Our first stop was at the hospital. Through the ever active but seldom precise grapevine we had heard there were openings for social workers there. We filled out the application forms in the corner of an office, full of hope, then saw the secretary stack them on an inch-high pile of similar applications. "We'll let you know," she said, closing the door behind us.

Outside, the air was full of the first tinges of the thick golden autumn sunlight. Among the flower beds the insects droned heavily, nearing their end. Any day now there would be a freeze.

We sat in the truck staring straight ahead but making no effort to move for a while. "What next?" Jack asked.

"There's an ad in the paper for a secretary at the college," I said. "And an assistant in the library."

"Okay. I'll drop you off there and go on over to the welfare office. They seem to hire almost anybody."

We made our separate rounds. At the college, the personnel manager was cordial but shocked that someone with a master's degree should be applying for a secretary's job.

"It's been our experience," she said, tapping the paper before her with her pencil, "that underemployed people aren't happy with their work for long."

"Underemployed?"

"Yes. People who have more education or qualifications than the job requires."

"Better underemployed than unemployed."

"Perhaps," she answered vaguely.

Jack's experience at the welfare office had been as unproductive. "I filled out the forms, but there was a backlog a mile long." We chugged mournfully along the road home.

The next day Jack went further afield to Santa Fe. "Don't wait up for me," he said. "I may have to stay over to get around to all the places."

I spent the day hoeing in a desultory fashion, picking a few beans, watching the bees crawl over the last of the clover. But everything seemed to fall from my hands after a while. I couldn't grasp hold of work firmly when I was expecting it to be snatched away at any moment. What was happening now, across the mountains in Santa Fe? Any luck? Any job? The prospect of leaving the farm was enough to unnerve me. But what if no job at all appeared? What then? We were, at long last, at the end of our rope.

The night was long. I watched the moon rise and make its arc across the blackness above, as I had lain by the window and watched it often before. I always knew now just what phase the moon was in, something I had never noticed much over a year ago. It was a strong light on our sonorro, often strong enough to cast shadows and efface the light of the stars around it. If I had to leave here, the moon would be taken away from me.

It was dark again the next evening before Jack came pulling into the yard. His suit was wrinkled by now and the knees had smudges on them.

"Car trouble," he explained, "as usual."

I set before him the supper I had kept warm in the oven and waited.

"No luck," he said. "At least nothing definite. I went to every school in Santa Fe. Even the prison. They had an opening for a teacher there. But I don't think. . . . Maybe . . ." He got up and went outside, leaving his supper half finished.

The next day we didn't go anywhere. Jack suffered the same ennui I felt. He would pick up a stone and then let it fall in confusion from his hands. Would we ever live in that house? It didn't seem worth the effort to do anything at all. So we sat in the sunshine and tried to think of new ways of phrasing the old question: what shall we do now?

In the afternoon one of the little Chavez girls came timidly up to the gate. "Can you come to the telephone?" she asked. "Someone wants you." We both sprung up, vacillating between hope and fear.

"I didn't give the Chavez phone number on any of the applications," Jack said. "What can it mean?"

He dashed off down the road after the little girl. Thirty minutes later he came back whooping.

"A job," he cried. "A job!"

A friend of ours, knowing our plight, had suggested us as consultants for a federally funded project in town. A short-term affair—only three months—but good money while it lasted. Almost physically the weight of fear fell off us. The children laughed and shouted. Mentally I began to pack.

The next day was Sunday. Some friends from a farm further up the river came and took the goats away. Maisie was just as obstinate about leaving as she had been about coming here. But after we coaxed her two curious golden children into the back of the truck, she followed, albeit with much complaining. Matilda had to be cornered and carried away, a job that took most of the afternoon.

After the truck had rumbled away, we wandered up behind the house and sat down on an old wagon bed that was slowly disintegrating into the landscape. The sky was pink in the west. In the greying east the evening star grew brighter. Suarez's truck, surrounded by its phalanx of dogs, stopped down on the bridge. He crawled out and stood gazing down at the water, now flowing higher than at any time during the summer. Having satisfied himself that all was well, he climbed back in, whistled to the dog that rode beside him, and the truck lumbered slowly on home. Further down the road, the sound of the Chavez children playing in that final hour before bedtime came drifting pleasantly along the dusty road.

This was my home. That first spring night I had lain awake in the dark, wondering where I was. Now I knew this place as I had never known any other: all the trees, the weeds, the insects and animals. I knew the hard, reluctant dirt and how the water ran over it. When it would rain, when it would snow, when the wind would beat the dust into the air. When the river would turn muddy red and when it would flicker clear over the round rocks in its bed. I had filled notebooks with its description, a daily diary of weather and earth doings. Now it was over and gone. Or rather my sojourn here was over and gone. The sun would continue to go down over the purple mesas, the evening star glow in the east, and Suarez check the water in the ditch. But I would not be here. I had learned where I was only to leave it. To the land itself I was merely a passing acquaintance. It would shrug off every imprint of our story soon. Only the beginnings of the rock walls would remain, looking as much like ruins as beginnings.

Within a week we were packed and moving out. Wilson came down to see us off, angry and accusing. He insisted that we leave everything we had acquired since we came there, taking only what we had brought with us in the beginning. We were too worn out and overwhelmed with failure to argue with him.

"I should have known it wouldn't work," he said. "You're running out. Giving up."

"Wilson, we've tried to explain. There's this operation of Alice's. And you've given us no assurance about the land, that you'll sell any to us or make any arrangements."

"You expect me to make arrangements with people who give up?" he cried.

We knew then that it was hopeless, had been hopeless from the start.

The morning we hauled the last load away was bright and clear. We shut and locked the door and whistled to the dog. We bumped out through the gate and shut it again slowly, drawing the barbed wire loop tight over the skinned pole, savoring for the last time the sun soaking into the dry sonorro. We pulled past all the scattered adobe houses with the hollyhocks turning brown in the front yards. Out on the road a band of lean stray horses tore up slender mouthfuls of dry buffalo grass and stared at us with large, unconcerned eyes. They didn't have to leave. Sparse as their life was, they didn't have to leave.

8

Then he showed me the river of the water of life, bright as crystal, flowing from the throne of God and of the Lamb through the middle of the street of the city; also, on either side of the river, the tree of life . . . and the leaves of the tree were for the healing of the nations. There shall no more be anything accursed.

—Revelation 22:1–2

But now the detestable, gangrenous suburb I have to walk through, the workers' shacks with their peeling paint and permanent layers of dirt, the tool sheds sinking into the sewers and streams that reek of washing and toilets, and the corrugated iron that constitutes man's choicest building material—all are gone, transformed into a wall of pure gold, a new enclosure for the city, pierced by the river of living water, as by an eternal crystal.

—Jacques Ellul, *The Meaning of the City*

hen we had set out toward our new life five seasons before, we imagined that we were driving our pale blue pickup straight into the heart of the beatific vision. We believed we could escape the wrath to come simply by reentering the Garden of Delight. "Back to the land" has always meant "back to Eden." Back to that union with creation from which we have been severed but for which we have retained a taste through centuries of starvation. Even now, when only artificial environments are familiar to us and the "natural

138

world" has become something strange and exotic, even in this pitiable state, our heart's craving for creation is stronger than ever. So strong that we were ready to risk all we had, or thought we had, to slake that thirst.

We had, however, failed to reckon with the cherubim with the flaming sword guarding the entrance to Eden. Somehow for our age it is easy enough to believe in Eden, that repository for all pleasures where the twisted ambiguities of our lives are straightened out. But we forget about the forbidding cherubim. Instead, comic St. Peter acts as tour guide through those dusty jokes about heaven. Militant angels to exclude the enlightened? That wouldn't be fair.

If our parents—call them by whatever names you please—Adam and Eve or Mr. and Mrs. Middleclass— had fallen, made mistakes, chosen badly, how could that affect us? We couldn't be blamed for their transgressions. Yet we came smack up against the gates to the garden, and not only were we turned away, but the blow from the flaming sword still smarts to this day. We weren't simply refused admittance; in our attempt to storm the gates we were doomed to reenact every area of failure pronounced upon our ancestors. It was our story Genesis was telling.

We also, just as Eve, desired a tree to make us wise. This was in fact the very temptation to which we yielded in what is comfortably called "drug experiences" nowadays. We voraciously sought vision, insight, knowledge, through many labyrinthine ways—astrology, I Ching, yoga, fasting—and the result was always and ever only more self-consciousness. We discovered the same truth over and over: that we were naked. Defenseless, powerless, exposed to assaults from a hostile society and ungovernable nature. Treachery and betrayal between friends and lovers. Brokenness—untogetherness—within. The same curse that descended on Eve and Adam when they desired to become wise overwhelmed us also when we ingested chemicals promising that magical aura of illumination.

This is not intended to be a polemic against—or for— hallucinogenics. Like everything else in the natural world, like yoga or meditation or diets or fasting, they are merely raw material. They operated for us the way the Law worked for Paul in Galatians. They revealed our inadequacies and nakedness. That knowledge in itself is of very little value. Adam and Eve were better off before they needed fig leaves. Knowing you're naked can easily lead to paranoia, fear, distrust, contempt for the nakedness of others, especially if they're not quite so conscious of their condition as you. Simply because we had an avenue to expanded consciousness that most of our society feared (the appeal the serpent made was to venturesomeness), we were disdained by those who feared to look at their nakedness.

True, we glimpsed visions of surpassing loveliness, of intricacies and grandeur in the natural world humming around us. But these visions in themselves made impossible demands upon the seer: if the flow of life so lovely to behold was to go on uninterrupted, one must remain absolutely still so as not to break in upon the flow and destroy its natural pattern. As soon as we moved we were an intrusion, outsiders upsetting perfection. Thus the hours' long vigils on rocky hillsides watching an anthill, hardly daring to breathe lest an entire army of insects be crushed underfoot. To a cow, wiping out anthills was nothing, but to us, the knowledge that we were misfits in the universe was a continual bitterness.

Perhaps the healthiest wisdom we attained through eating of the cannabis tree and related species was a sense of how ridiculous we were. We spent hours around the table, around the stove, trucking over the rough ground, laughing like loons at ourselves and our complete incongruity in this world. Seeing the kitchen as a television stage, the sonorro as a movie set, memorizing Firesign Theatre records. Our actions were at least two removes from reality. It was hilariously funny, this dislocation of ours, and the tree of knowledge showed us just how funny.

And sometimes it showed us how scary. How tenuous was our out-of-place foothold upon this earth. How little it mattered to the buzzing, humming universe whether our foot slipped or not. Breaking our necks falling from a cliff or drowning in the red water of the river would mean as little as our disruption of the anthill. The cosmos would go imperturbably on, exploding and imploding. Eden had operated admirably, after all, without Adam.

So what if Adam hadn't been around to name the animals? The creatures had flourished nameless. Maisie and Matilda, Big Mama and Peter certainly loved us no more for giving them foolish names. They resisted us till the iron bar was laid to the back of their skulls or we shut them into someone else's truck and gratefully exchanged them for money. We did not resolve the enmity that was placed between humans and the rest of the animal world at Moriah. Accepting that breach as a part of agrarian life did not heal it. The cages, the fences, the ropes, the bee veils and smokers, the sporadic attempts at vegetarianism all testified to an oppression we had inherited from Adam.

Since our generation had been raised on a Disney version of creation, complete with talking animals, the serpent speaking to Eve in Eden came as no surprise. What shocked us was how our animals mistrusted us. Unlike Genesis, Disney doesn't prepare you for animal animosity. We loved our beasts of the field—at least the furry, warm-blooded ones—but we never learned to overcome their enmity. With all our hearts we believed a redeemed creation meant the lion and lamb would lie side by side in peace. But though we longed to learn Saint Francis's secret way with animals, our creatures relentlessly resisted us.

Our disappointment was tempered by one faint hope. We also believed, along with Walt Whitman, that animals "bring us tokens of ourselves." Because they are not cursed with self-consciousness or the capacity to deceive themselves like humans, they reflect reality more directly. Every animal we caged showed an innate urge to excape. Their watchful eyes, their ferocious struggles actually gave us hope that freedom was not an illusion. Their ardent yearning for escape kept the flavor of freedom alive for us as well.

In a world as deterministic as ours, it is easy not to believe in freedom anymore. Yet more than anything else the taste for freedom had called us out of the cages where we had lived so acquiescently. We wanted to break out of a society where the choices had already been made for us by shadowy powers that filled our feeders and water dishes regularly but checked the latch on the cage door just as unfailingly.

Choices and alternatives are not efficient. They slow down the machinery and make trouble for those responsible for keeping the wheels rolling. Yet it was the complicated and time-consuming sideroads that fascinated us. However, it was not only the rigidity of a relatively recent technological society that kept us bound. Our relationships with one another lacked an inner freedom, bound by a repetition of ages-old patterns that we seemed unable to break.

Nowhere was this more startlingly evident than in the relationships between men and women. We were aware of this particular curse but unable to overcome it. Theories and practical regimens for solving what the men called "the woman problem" multiplied and were modified daily. Friendships were possible; indeed they sometimes flourished, particularly between people of the same sex, drawn together by common interests, similar backgrounds, mutually compatible personalities. But it was exceedingly difficult for men and women to be friends, much less lovers, with any long-lived success. Suspicion and jealousy born of possessiveness marred even the simple sensual pleasure of reciprocal sexual desire. The object of passion was either completely oblivious to the subject, or else twisted the situation to his or her own advantage.

This situation, I believe, was especially bitter for the women. They might discount Eve's curse in Genesis, but they were painfully aware of Freud's restatement of it: biology is destiny. If they had succeeded in circumventing the first part of the curse—*in grief you shall bear children*—the second part still rankled enough to produce profound misery. The dilemma was this: any man, given the chance, would "lord it over" a woman. Yet in satisfying sexual desires, how does one avoid that distinct possibility? Desire, fear, and resentment tore at every woman there. The more exotic alternatives—notably lesbianism and nymphomania—were as fraught with danger as plain old vanilla sexual exploitation. We may have talked bravely about settling for "mere sex," but we all found it impossible and not really satisfactory to disentangle our affections from our genitals.

Men, I think, are usually unwitting pawns in this particular curse. True, this Genesis story was first spoken in a culture that, without much thought, relegated women

144

to the status of property. Which makes the story all the more fascinating. It took some supracultural revelation to show that women were indeed responsible moral agents. Otherwise, how could Eve have played such a large and tragic part in this primeval drama? It is her curse that Adam acts out his now "natural" inclination to oppress. But if this truly were the "order of creation" in its paradisal state, we would have to say that enmity, grief, and shame were also a part of paradise. The oppression of women by men is a curse to be cured, not a creation to be glorified.

Nevertheless, it was not cured at Moriah. It festered, produced divisions and distrust. And it was one of the principal causes of our dissolution. The insatiable desire for true sexual union went on unabated by one disappointment after another. When all the sexual possibilities were exhausted within the community, people tended to move on. And for the pair of us who were linked together as one flesh, it was time to move closer. Biology was indeed destiny in a way Freud perhaps never suspected. The ancient curse had to be dealt with day by day.

And day by day mouths had to be fed. And work had to be done. And of course there were those who refused to put their hand to the plow, perhaps because they were already looking back.

If there was ever a land cursed with thorns and thistles, it was northern New Mexico, armed with cactus and cockleburs. Much of the curse was the direct result of the interference of man. This barren country had not always been so. Western Europeans had laid it waste, just as Africans had made a desert of the Sahara. And we labored under the burden of their rapacity—sweating, ignorant of the ways of the land, only slowly learning how to bring forth anything other than thorns and thistles.

And the curse on the ground didn't end there. This land we loved even in its barrenness, that we slowly learned to work with, was in the end denied us. The illusion that the earth can be owned infected both our vision and Wilson's, as it had Don Juan Oñate's before us. Friendship and community were destroyed by the accursed concept of possession.

We have dragged the rest of creation down with us, despoiled it of its original beauty, made it merely an attribute of ourselves. Actually, the greatest virtue in living on the land is the way it makes one aware of our true state outside the garden; we live at the mercy of the rest of creation, dependent on it. It is easy enough in a city apartment to live as though we had indeed subdued the very weather. The farmer at least knows better.

In reading over various Utopian fantasies that have from time to time beguiled the human imagination, from Plato's *Republic* to Skinner's *Walden Two*, I am struck by what is the central concern of them all: the division of labor and the ownership of property. They have all rightly identified property possession as a great evil, corrupting the basis of human community. All devised schemes for circumventing this evil. Plato proposed a "royal lie" to be told to the growing crop of guardians: they themselves grew out of the earth and are made of gold and therefore have no need of property that satisfies the common herd. Voltaire had the idea of making chamberpots and fetters out of gold and silver to reduce their value, and H. G. Wells made the World State "the sole landowner of the earth." Yet all these schemes seem incredibly naive now.

The problem of work is an even bigger muddle among Utopians. They saw that property ownership is in itself unnatural, even if their cures are quackery. But work, which Genesis specifically identifies as a curse upon humanity, this curse the Utopians have sweated to make a virtue. Work is not a matter of amusing oneself, as Francis Bacon would have it in his *New Atlantis,* where the Renaissance scientist, dressed up as Solomon, putters around his laboratory. At least B. F. Skinner was realistic in prescribing more work-credits for disagreeable drudgery than for titillating research.

Work is not prayer; it is one of those things we have learned to call so glibly a "necessary evil." For it is not the exertion of muscles nor the devouring of time that is at the heart of this curse, but the stark contingency of our position on this earth. We must eat. We live on a treadmill of necessity. No fruit drops, unaided, into our hand. Even the hunters-and-gatherers of this world, the aborigines, live in such an attenuated paradise that few of us would share it with them.

Although those idlers who sat in the house all day at Moriah playing records or telling jokes on the front steps were ignorant of the Shorter Catechism, they were not fooled into thinking that the chief end of man was work, even if they were more intent on enjoying themselves than on enjoying God.

But then Utopias have never spared much room or time on idlers. Their designers feel acutely the mess human society is in. They see the dilapidated ruin into which we have fallen. But their answer has been a nail here and a patch there to shore up the ruins. And Utopias don't allow much freedom.

Utopias are almost always discovered through some shipwreck or time-machine malfunction. Or else, as with Plato or Skinner, they are the result of sheer futurology fantasy. But the most ideal human societies actually discovered and described by anthropologists and attested to by old-fashioned empirical evidence—say the Mesolithic Caribou Eskimos of central Canada or the recently unearthed Tasaday tribe in the Philippines, where gentle concern for the common welfare is put before all else—who among us would actually go and join them? Our reluctance would no doubt spring from some small quibble about dirt or diet.

Here and there in hidden places on the earth exist these dwindling bands of humans who accept with humility the fragile precariousness of the space they occupy. But expose them for only a few days to outside influences and see which is stronger in this world—sickness or health. Aboriginal people are quickly infected by the curses we carry.

In the end it is the dust that owns us all. Some peoples, usually those not insulated from the contingencies of life, submit to this final, uncontrollable happenstance with a grace we find difficult to understand. The stoicism I developed at Moriah did not serve me well when it came to death. It was easy enough to be stoical about the limp rabbit bodies that Jack so deftly skinned. Even if the sight was unpleasant, we always ate the tasty flesh. We learned to accept the death of farm animals. But when death crept nearer and reached its stilling hand into the very spring of human life, our philosophies were undone. The birth of a dead child was the final contradiction, the last denial.

Yet even with the curse, mercy makes life possible. If Adam and Eve insisted on knowing their nakedness, God provided the clothing to cover it. The consequence was not cancelled, merely made bearable. With Eve's pain, he multiplied her pleasure, and if work is not a virtue, it is at least at times a consolation. Thus the curse is tempered.

We had been played out on a line, allowed to imagine that we had escaped the exigencies that affect ordinary mortals; and then with a snag that tore open the skin of our dreams, we were hauled back in to grasp the chill, harsh wind of reality.

———

A month after we left Moriah and moved into a rundown but respectable neighborhood in town, we were struggling to our financial feet with the aid of our federal project jobs. Yet we were still spiritually desperate. Our agrarian dreams had dwindled to the size of our bare, packed-dirt yard where we halfheartedly sowed some grass seed. Our one remaining rabbit, poor Furball, was stolen by neighborhood boys and rescued down by the railroad track at the very moment they were about to hit it over the head with a bottle. The glorious autumn that had been full of high winds and apple picking and harvest the year before now filled only the narrow sky above our house. Our dog, ignorant of city ways, was run over and injured. Our friends had scattered, some of them still sick, almost all as disconsolate as ourselves. We were outside the gate of

Eden, the sword at our backs, not knowing which path to take away from the garden.

The house echoed with its emptiness. Without our discarded furniture and possessions, we hadn't even those familiar consolations. It was in every way a shabby and makeshift life. Sensing that this could only be an interim, a breathing space between the failure we'd left behind and an unknown future, our girls were uneasy and troubled. What next, they asked mutely.

Jack and I felt secure only at work, where everything was scheduled and programmed. But at night we couldn't sleep and clung together in the darkness, full of fear and anxiety. We were at our last extremity. We didn't know the answer to our children's question.

Alice had her operation. She was frightened, but as was her habit, tried not to show it. I sat by her bed and watched her waken groggily, mistrustfully, from the anesthetic. While she was recuperating at home, I read to her in the afternoons the whole series of the Narnia books of C. S. Lewis, stories of a marvelous kingdom beyond our grimy time and space where adventure and heroism were still possible. The children could not devour enough of these stories—Lewis says that youth has a natural appetite for heaven—and as for me, my own jaundiced palate began to tingle again with the longing for Something More. If only I too could somehow slip into a world where something mattered again. When we came to *The Silver Chair,* I recognized the sensation of living underground for so long that the sun itself seemed a myth. The torpor and cynicism that had bitten deep into Prince Rilian had settled into my bones too. I thought of Dostoyevsky's underground man. Better not to live than be like that.

Jack and I had followed our dream into the desert and found it to be no more than a mirage. I couldn't stand a second disappointment like that. Besides, I had nothing left with which to stake a second claim. All my resources—physical, financial, spiritual—had been exhausted. Jack and I were exceptionally gentle towards one another but with the sympathy one invalid might show for another.

About three blocks straight down the street from our house sat a church we had often passed, initially as the town's first hippies, later as honey peddlers and clinic visitors, and most recently as respectably disguised researchers for the government. The name of the minister on the signboard was Gotheim. I had often mentally sneered at such a German name in an overwhelmingly Hispanic culture. Other than that, I had given the building no attention at all. But now that my desperation was acute and no other path presented itself, I decided to venture down the three blocks—as tentatively as possible, in case another painful disappointment should be lurking in the little white stucco building.

What else could I expect but to have my suspicions confirmed? This or any other American church was no more than a travesty of certain high principles long since betrayed by centuries of distortion and neglect. What was the use of even wrestling with the question of whether or not Jesus was who he claimed to be? What difference had it made if he were God himself or in some mysterious way related to him? Jesus hadn't changed the world after all. Everything I valued teetered on the brink of destruction, the forces of Evil so palpable I could feel them crowding in and smothering me. Surely Evil would ultimately collapse under its own weight; that was its nature. But after that, what? Nothingness? Annihilation? I believed in Evil as I believed in nothing else. Its power was apparent in our own failure. We were helpless against it. Hadn't Jesus been just as powerless?

Still, whether from desperation or the hunger sharpened by those children's stories, I decided to try this little church. No, it wasn't even a conscious decision, just a growing resolve.

I said nothing at all to my unsuspecting family, simply got up one Sunday morning, put on my most unobtrusive career clothes, and made myself presentable for Presbyterians. When I finally explained to the girls, with considerable embarrassment, where I was going, they were excited, not realizing that my trepidation was greater than when I'd started for New Mexico. They insisted on dressing up and going with me. Jack said nothing, only looked at me with bewilderment. But when I reached the middle of the last block, I saw him coming along behind us, his hands thrust deeply into the pockets of his grey suit and his head down. We reached the church just as the ushers were closing the doors after the last stragglers and the music had begun.

To describe that place today is like trying to describe the details of one's first realization of home. Or like being at the bottom of a deep well. It was dark and the sounds echoed. And the well was filled with half-forgotten associations collected and distilled over months of Sundays: the self-conscious swish of best clothes, the polished, dark-stained pews, the ornate iron heat registers, the careful sacred silence broken by whispers and coughs and crying babies, the chilled church air gradually warmed by the gathering bodies standing, sitting, pumping out the Gloria and Doxology.

People gather nowhere else on earth in the same strange spirit as when they worship. The air was charged with a multifold attention struggling to direct itself, to be taken up into, if only momentarily, Something More. The polka dots on the dress in front of me filled me with strange elation. The shoulders shifted under them and then straightened. Who knew what problems this woman brought with her, who exposed her nakedness, despite the polka dots, to the one who walked in the garden at evening and said, "Where are you?" She had three boys sitting beside her who alternately poked at one another and turned and stared at us. When we stood to sing, the youngest leaned against his mother and she absently put an arm around him and patted his shirt front in time with the music.

The songs were like water in my parched mouth; I wrapped my tongue around delicious words that had to be drawn a long way up from the well of my memory. No one there, I felt, made the responses—"Lord, have mercy, Christ, have mercy"—out of such a deep wound as I did.

If the gathered faithful ever caught a sense of the wild, desperate hope with which strangers at times approach their familiar sanctuary, perhaps they would recapture their own sense of deliverance from danger instead of sinking into cozy boredom.

There was nothing extraordinary about the service, no trendy gimmicks to appeal to the disaffected. The traditional hymns were played by a greying organist. The choir was enthusiastically dreadful. I can recall neither the text nor the sermon, except that the words of the Scripture affected me like one who has not heard his native tongue spoken for years. It was not slogans, not jargon, not rhetoric, nor the deliberately leveled communication of the professional proletarian. It was language, elevated, elusive, drawing the hearer on and into its depth.

In contrast, the minister groped and stumbled, shifted syntax in mid-sentence, mispronounced, and muttered. Yet that detracted nothing. He was obviously excited about what he was saying; he attempted to hide none of his deficiencies and, what was more, seemed undismayed by them. They were entirely beside the point. His own nakedness had deepened to transparency.

It was all over too soon, the rustling bulletins, the hymnbooks plopping in the racks at the final threefold Amen. We shuffled through the handshaking line, the children staring up in frank wonderment at the unfamiliar faces. The minister was not the thin, pale missionary type I had expected, but rotund and red as any Martin Luther, his open black robe snagged at the sleeve and frayed at the collar. People were naturally curious about us, but they concealed it with as good a grace as possible.

This was the first salve on our raw sores we had felt in many a day. I tried picking about, as we walked home, for signs of a false comfort that came from once more having been among the secure bourgeoisie. But I soon gave that up. Besides the fact that several people had seemed definitely on the outskirts of financial well-being, I had simply enjoyed the release from my own torturing anxieties too much to analyze the experience.

We were, in fact, all disgustingly, Sunday-afternoon happy. The girls skipped ahead of us like something out of Dick and Jane. Jack and I had a long, leisurely afternoon nap, and then we went back that night for the potluck supper, carrying our contribution of two loaves of freshly baked whole wheat bread. This time I was more scared. It was one thing to sit in a church service among these people and quite another to make conversation with them over macaroni casseroles and green chili and chocolate cupcakes. They were the insiders, used to the well-worn jokes and able to identify each dish with its maker. The waves of common humanness and hospitality that washed about them, however, lapped up against us too. We sat with a biology professor and his wife. They had grown children, he told us wryly, folding and refolding his napkin, off somewhere seeing the world, experimenting. The conversation was awkward but possible. Somehow I made no unreasonable demands upon it. I felt sorry for these parents, resigned to not understanding their children. They were as real as I was.

This was only the beginning, of course, of a life together. Just so, lovers look back in amazement at their first meeting and laugh at the silly, inconsequential things that attracted them to one another. Fortified with food and fellowship with people we had long ago written off as insignificant, we walked home in the brittle autumn darkness. After we put the girls to bed, Jack and I talked, hesitantly, awkwardly, about the day and its experiences. There was no denying its genuineness. There had been no razzmatazz to attract us with its innovativeness; just a certain stark homeliness. No back-slapping exuberance that I remembered only too well from earlier times, but a courteous curiosity and openness. Was it possible that in such an unlikely place lived a health stronger than our sickness? We were almost afraid to hope.

We felt as if we were emerging from the underground and discovering, somewhat like Prince Rilian, that the Son was not a myth after all. And our first inkling of this was the light and warmth we had felt that day. No matter what the theoretical pros and cons of such an unlikely story as the defeat of Death and the prospect of living under blessing rather than curse, that day we had touched, heard, eaten, and drunk its evidence. To deny the mending and healing we could feel at work within us would be to deny our own senses.

We were as avid to follow this new hope, once we were convinced of its authenticity, as we had been to follow our dream to New Mexico. We asked the minister to visit us, and when he did, we barraged him with questions and information about our predicament. I think he was surprised at finding other people as excitable as he was, to whom faith in God's gracious and powerful purpose was a matter of life and death. Had our weary failures been, after all, not in vain? Had it been necessary for us to travel those subterranean ways in order to emerge in this place?

It is hard for anyone whose life has begun again to contain—or sustain—that first joy. The sense of living in a cosmic drama exhilarates, almost intoxicates. We say we want our lives to have meaning. Yet when the fact they do dawns upon us, we can scarcely stand under the weight of the implications.

Neither was the journey over. If we had always been traveling, even if unwittingly, toward this place of recognition and clarity, it was itself but a point on a pilgrimage that stretched before us. A pilgrimage that is absolutely unpredictable. Just like Bunyan's Christian on his journey, we were faced with the same decisions all over again every day. Our quest was part of a pattern that did not end with a final flourish that Sunday in October. Following that we spent a year as hired hands on a mountain ranch where we recollected ourselves, read, and became more inquisitive than ever before about our faith.

During that year, the knowledge grew in us that the next step on our journey was seminary. That meant another three years to work out how we were going to give an account of the hope that was in us. At one time, four years would have seemed an eternity of waiting. The apocalypse was already upon us. But the true relativity of time is revealed when you finally realize that you are not writing the script to the cosmic drama, but merely acting out your part in fidelity to its author. Last week the same biology professor with whom we sat at that fateful potluck table was the first to lay his hands on Jack's head at his ordination.

Last week also, Patricia Hearst, Emily and Jack Harris, and Wendy Yoshimura were arraigned in California courts, members of that other apocalyptic community, the Symbionese Liberation Army. I look at their pictures, read their statements, follow with fascination and fear the unfolding of their story. Because I know that the same road that took our caravan out of the Midwest several years ago could as easily have ended in the court as in the sanctuary. Only a fraction more of separation from society, perhaps a permanent disavowal from a parent, a solitary act of arrogant authority by the police, an unwarranted arrest, only one straw more and the social contract between ourselves and American society could have been irrevocably broken. We too could have become guerrillas in an underground army for whom to die violently is itself victory. We too might have laid hold of the kingdom of God by violence. Just such zealots, advocates of righteous violence, were numbered among Christ's own disciples.

But thin, spidery threads of grace held us back from the final rupture: the concern of the public health nurse, the obvious mental anguish of the food stamp official, even the postmistress at the next village who gave us her windfall apples. And also our own fear and revulsion for irrational violence, which was a more or less constant threat to us at Moriah, whether from drunks who cruised around the back roads in their own desperation or from businessmen sweating out their fantasies in their cars and hoping to pick up a compliant hitchhiker. Society was our adversary as surely as it was Noah's. And only those unnoticed accumulations of small graces restrained us from attacking our adversary with the weapons it knows and understands only too well.

Despite the dangers, though, there was something of solid value in the Moriah experience, even with its futility, despair, and dead-end conclusion. It provided a stark and unavoidable confrontation with anguish, with unmitigated failure, that in other situations can easily be lied about, covered over, or distracted from. Moriah made clear to me what being an exile from Eden means in a society that pretends, simultaneously, that there is no such place and that we have never left it.

I also learned some remarkable things about myself. For example, I had always pictured myself as easygoing and undemanding, the world's most inoffensive person. At Moriah I learned differently. I made tremendous demands on people. Contracting to live in the same household with me was like entering a monastery, only the rules were sprung on the unsuspecting novitiates after they had been led to believe they were on a holiday cruise. I demanded renunciation of all other loyalties, consecration of all one's energies to my particular dream, recognition of my superior discipline and austerity. Pounded daily upon the solidity of reality, my image of myself began to crumble. I was someone very different than I had thought. One would suppose that this kind of learning could be a little easier come by. But if I had not had seventeen people instead of three telling me what I was like at close quarters, perhaps I never would have learned. Illusions break up on the rocks of reality, and how fortunate that they do. If we were inventing our own story, what a sad little meaningless tale it would be.

We learned another very important thing at Moriah: how to be poor. Poverty is viewed as the single greatest sin in our society. It is an enemy to be annihilated, a shame to be hidden. Whether springing from the conservative sources that say success is a sign of God's favor or from liberal sources that say we must all enter the heaven of the median income, the message is the same: we must be saved from poverty. But one has experiences when one is poor that are forever denied to insulated society, hermetically sealed in financial security. Of course, like anything else, like drugs or education or geography, poverty is raw material. It can be just as easily subverted as wealth, making its subject spiteful, petty, brutal. But in our society, the positive potential of poverty has been obscured. We scoff at its romantic advocates, pity its victims, ignore its Teacher.

I learned from poverty what I could learn from no other school. I learned not to rely on possessions to supply an identity. When you drive up to the bank in a rattletrap truck with slick tires and try to cash a check that you pull out of a worn flannel pocket with fingers permanently blackened from soot and axle grease, you learn to be prepared for people who don't believe in you; yet even against that heavy wall of denial, you know your own worth. You learn to stare down the insolent eyebrows of other customers who pay cash when you pull out your food stamps, refusing to accept their ignorant estimate of yourself and knowing that we all ultimately live by welfare and grace. And, if you are very lucky, you learn how close to the edge all human life is lived, how we are held in existence from moment to moment by a power we don't control. You can rejoice in life as a gift. In poverty there is no pretense and no protection.

The church became for us the fully fleshed reality of that phantom community that always recedes just over the horizon, always eluding our grasp. The amazing thing was that the same sorts of dreadful people who had wandered through Moriah inhabited the church. Untrustworthy, petty, irresponsible, lazy, bad-tempered, demanding, manipulative. On top of that, most of them were decidedly middle class and had no aspirations to be otherwise. Quite a few drove offensively large cars, ate meat without a qualm, and voted Republican. Some were alcoholics; some were neurotics; some were simply boring. Still they came together regularly for the specific purpose of being judged. Their failures and inadequacies were weekly pointed out to them. They were exposed, naked before one another. And though they writhed or sighed or denied, they seldom fell into despair. They accepted with joy or wry bewilderment the mystery of forgiveness that was just as regularly placed before them.

They were a redeemed community, or at least they were continually told they were, even if they didn't often feel like it. And if the realization of their redemption lay in the future and was as yet only dimly perceived, still there were enough flashes of fulfillment and foretaste to keep alive the hope.

A chemist scoffed at the moldy notion of angelic choirs in heaven; he was the choir director. Alongside him was a Chicano volunteer worker on welfare who sweated out his own private chemistry of alcoholism. An elderly schoolteacher, fretful in retirement, morbidly afraid of falling on her stairs and not being discovered for days. A couple who faced divorce over the heads of their unsuspecting children. And the old, grime-encrusted, palsied half-wit who showed up Sunday after Sunday, shoveling in quantities of food at the potlucks; he was there because it was a place where he could shake hands with half a hundred people who knew his name.

None of these were people I would have chosen to set up an "intentional community" with. Few, if any, shared my radical political views. They were confused, frightened, pained by the chaos and change that whirled them around like flotsam in its rush. But their reality was as solid as mine, and the community we formed together was more solid than any of us.

Christians today experience a very meager diet of communal life for the most part, a few hours a week at best. But enclaves exist, especially among Roman Catholics, which having tasted liturgical community, seek something more. Thus we have monasteries, convents, Protestant and ecumenical communes of various sorts. What of their efficacy and future?

Donald Bloesch in *Wellsprings of Renewal* described a veritable smorgasbord of contemporary Christian communal efforts, manifesting a multitude of tastes. But to enter upon any of these ventures is an exceedingly dangerous undertaking. To enter a monastery, one must take a series of vows, graduated in their seriousness and timespan. No less serious should be the commitment of Protestants entering a communal discipline. It will be a task more difficult than anything the novice has tried before. A person having trouble with marriage shouldn't try to assuage the pain by entering a commune, which is a magnified marriage. Someone dedicated primarily to self-development or personal growth shouldn't join a commune, where the survival of the community requires daily crucifixion of private desire. The body cannot long sustain an overgrown eye or ear or foot.

I would almost say no American should enter a commune. We have been trained for competition, personal achievement, rewards, recognition as a way of life. That cultural conditioning makes up such a large portion of our personality that we would be a gaping hole without it. If that hole is not filled with a substance stronger than cultural conditioning, the effort will be futile and guilt-ridden.

I must also warn myself against this great and dangerous discipline of communal life. The discipline of being a part of an ordinary church, one that periodically appears and disappears like atomic particles, is almost insupportable for all of us at times. Locally we are torn by petty considerations, such as what color to paint the kitchen or whether or not the choir should process. Globally we are torn by the same stupid questions put to Jesus by the first disciples—where shall we find bread for the multitudes and what do you mean by the kingdom of God anyway? I can foresee a lifetime of learning to live in this querulous community.

In fact, to admit the final humiliating truth, as long as I have my own family, I don't feel the need for anything more than those intermittent flashes of community. Hell, says Sartre, that preeminent existentialist, is other people. Heaven, replies C. S. Lewis, is an acquired taste. And some of us have to go through Hell to get there.

"The kingdom of God is hard enough," I protest, "and now you pile on top of that the Body of Christ. What do you expect of me anyhow?"

"Something more."

And how do I explain my life now? When exactly, at what point, did it become different? Does the little girl baptized on her eighth Easter so many years ago have no part in this story? Was her act unconsidered, of no account, not efficacious? Or did it mark the person I am forever, no matter how I tried to conceal, slough off, disguise my inscribed identity even to myself? For at no time did it occur to me to actively renounce that Christ I had been baptized into, any more than I would have disowned any other friend, though I despised his disfigured representations. I was a lost sheep wandering through the valley of that dark shadow, but one who had been branded at baptism with an ineradicable mark.

One can with perhaps more rationality attribute the reversal of my life to the early childhood education I received in the church rather than to the mystical experience of baptism, and I would be the last to discount it, although I am not at all sure that what I learned was what the Sunday school thought it was teaching. What I learned in church and what was grafted to me by my baptism was radical behavior. Unconventional, giving-up-everything, throwing-it-all-over behavior. And though I lost almost everything else, I never lost that vague, buried sense of loyalty to an absent Friend.

I have in this story tried to chart the nadir, to isolate the lowest point on the graph and the moment when the line began its upward movement. Certainly the story is now often full of great gobbets of pure sweetness. At times I sustain a continual state of gratitude, often for days on end. Great joy springs from this current of gratitude, which is at the same time wonder at my life and its continuing creation directly from the hand of God.

Yet doubtful, depressed, unfruitful interludes interrupt this flow. I would not be mapping this Christian path with the painstaking accuracy it demands if I denied that. There are times when all the beauty and bliss of early morning light absorbed by a glowing curl of orange peel and shimmering on the steam from the coffee cup transforms, by some horror, into smears of mess and disorder, husks from which the meaning has been sucked. At such moments, which stretch themselves into days, even weeks, the line on the graph plummets off the page.

I call these the times of obedience, when we are left without a reason why, without a meaning, just as Eve had no real reason given to her to explain why she shouldn't eat the fruit of the tree of knowledge. At those times we don't remain obedient in order to feel joyful or fulfilled or positive; usually we feel only a dull ache at best. We remain faithful, even though the words we pray are dust in our mouths, because we have a Lord of our lives, not a beneficent Behaviorist who doles out rewards as positive reinforcement.

And now, instead of the boredom of empty Sunday afternoons, we have fullness of life, sometimes to the point where we stagger under its weight. Boredom is not depression but flight from it. Boredom knows nothing of battles with dark forces because it will not stay and fight. Indeed it has no reason to fight, no weapons to fight with. And if the lives of my own particular saints are any indication, there will be an age of fighting. Luther's later years were filled with his worst depressions, C. S. Lewis' last nights with terror and nightmares.

But there are also now the times of protection and praise. We have in our house healing and a communion that is holy. All of us, even our animals, rejoice in one another. We say often to ourselves, "Isn't that just like her?" or "You get that from your father." A taste, a shadow of the perfected reality of communing saints.

———

Israel believed, above all else, in a God who interferes. Who comes walking in the evening and wants to know where you are. Who confused the tongues at Babel. Who arranged for Sarah's unexpected pregnancy. Who took an unwarranted liking to Nineveh. Who allowed Job to be toyed with. And who, as Christians further believe, having dabbled about in human affairs for a couple of thousand years, decided to make himself clear in Jesus Christ.

The medieval romancers, much cleverer than we at seeing connections, made stories about the Holy Rood, the cross, which originally grew untouched in Eden and was later used for the mast of Noah's ark. And at the end of the story, described in the Apocalypse of John, the tree of life, left behind so long ago in Eden, now stands in the Holy City awaiting the time when "there shall be no more curse." Thus the tree of death becomes for us the great reversal, the tree of life.

We are all of us somewhere on that long road that runs from the gate of Eden, closed forever to human habitation, to the gate of the New Jerusalem that stands perpetually open to receive the glory and honor of nations. And along each part of the road wander pilgrims.

A part of *our* journey led through Babylon, that seductive city that attempts to disguise itself as Jerusalem in order to win the allegiance of ardent seekers. But one must heed the call to come out of Babylon if one wants to journey on to the real Jerusalem.

Yet, having left Eden and Babylon behind, we still stood desolate on the road. Our Emmaus lay ahead.

Moving along toward it, we were like the disappointed disciples of a reformer, a martyred zealot, he whom they had hoped "should have redeemed Israel." But the one walking beside us turns out to be, not Ché Guevara after all, but something better. Something More. Not one bound to repeat the same old patterns of power and betrayal. But one who did what we, since Eve and Adam, can never do, fully unite his will to God's.

So from Emmaus we set out once more. The road didn't end there for Cleopas and his friend, and neither did it for us. It led back to the city and in amongst the other disciples. Together we seek to build an ark for our own apocalyptic times, a community that will see us through our forty days and nights of chaos and storm, as we strain our sight for the return of the dove.